Get the Job: Optimize Your Resume for the Online Job Search

By

Pamela Paterson

12/13

Although this book is intended to provide
information that is helpful and accurate, there is no
representation or warranty, express or implied, of
any kind regarding it. There is no guarantee
regarding the information's currency or accuracy,
or the currency or accuracy of information
contained on sites to which this book provides
links. This book may be used for information
purposes only and should expert advice be needed,
the services of a qualified professional should be
obtained. The author and the publisher disclaims
all liability of any kind whatsoever arising out of
your use of, or inability to use, this information.

ISBN-13: 978-1489524980

Writer Types Inc., Toronto, Canada,
www.writertypes.com

Edited by Tracey Grozier and Robert Long

Images by Carla Austin

What People Are Saying

"A Tremendous Help"

"I haven't written a resume since I finished school 20 years ago. I had added to it over the years, but when I found myself on the wrong side of a merger, my resume really looked like it was 20 years old. Pamela's advice on what to emphasize, and how to structure and lay out the resume to enable the key points to stand out was a tremendous help. Following Pamela's tips, I had a modern, professional-looking resume that I was very confident in sending out. In short order, I had calls and subsequently contracts coming in."

—T. Hendriks, Google Deployment Specialist

"A Piece of Gold"

"This resume book is a piece of gold for job seekers. It is the first resume book I have found that actually provides practical tips that are easy to understand and follow, and really work. Many resume books are unfortunately highly theoretical, and leave the job seeker in a cloud of confusion. Not so with Ms. Paterson's book, because as a natural writer and teacher, she has turned the book into a classroom and easily conveyed excellent tips in resume writing. She has provided an entire methodology in resume writing that will greatly benefit job seekers."

—C. Carajan, IT Manager

"A Fantastic Book"

"This is a fantastic book. Pamela did a great job in making resume tips very easy to understand. Even people with no practical writing experience will be able to pick this book up and use it to create an effective resume. As a senior staffing consultant who helps clients and candidates, even I found useful tips that I can pass along to my candidates."

—J. Gibson, Staffing Consultant

"Clear Way of Communicating"

"Pamela has a clear way of communicating information to people in a way that makes it immediately applicable to their needs. I have also asked her to present to my students and clients on workshops related to resumes and job finding skills. Her knowledge and effectiveness in transferring it to others is wonderful, and she can take subjects and make them come to life. Students often follow up with praise for Pamela and thanks to me for bringing her into the classroom to provide valuable lessons that can be applied right away to the job search!"

—B. Aschwanden, President, Publishing Smarter

"Practical Tips and Real Life Experience"

"I attended Pamela's webinar on resume writing with 15 of my graduating students and boy were we all happy we did! She shared a lot of practical tips and real life experiences to bring home the points she was making. I was also very happy that she had her participants mail her their resumes in advance and she took the time and effort to go through each resume and highlight the good, the bad and the ugly—a great learning experience indeed."

—S. Nene, Instructor, George Brown College

"Offered a Position That Was Perfect for Me"

"I recently moved to a metropolitan area and was looking for employment. I had virtually no experience with job boards or recruiters. In a small town environment, my current resume format would have landed me an interview, but applying for jobs in a large highly competitive market meant that response to that version of my resume posted on major job boards was sporadic at best, resulting in opportunities presented to me that were not even relevant to my skill set. After meeting with Pamela and revising my resume, I immediately posted the new version...and **literally within 3 hours I received two calls from recruiters about appropriate opportunities. The next day was spent fielding responses from more than 12 recruiters for more than 15 positions**—all of which were relevant to my skill set! Within 2 weeks I had interviews, and within 3 weeks was offered a position that was perfect for me. I received unsolicited comments from both interviewers and recruiters as to the professionalism of my newly revised resume, and how impressive it was. I credit Pamela for her insight into what works, what doesn't, and what is needed to create a winning and effective resume."

—P. Cruickshank, Technical Writer

Contents

Chapter 3: Create Layout and Design 13

About This Book

Paul had been looking for a job for eight months. When he applied the resume writing techniques in this book, he found a job in one week.

"Congratulations! You got the job."

Introduction

Paul called me and asked for help with his resume. Paul was a documentation and usability professional who had been unemployed for eight months. He had impressive qualifications—a master's degree from a top university and work experience with a prominent politician—but none of it helped him get a job.

I could see how the weight of unemployment was pushing Paul down. When I extended my hand to meet him, Paul rose from his slouched position in the chair as if every move he made just required energy he didn't have. When he shook my hand, I felt depleted in that brief moment our palms met. He had nothing left.

Paul also had a major disability to deal with. He was in a car accident, which left him visually impaired. His eyes were very sensitive to the fluorescent light in the coffee shop, which he handled by alternating between two pairs of glasses: on and off, off and on.

Paul and I reviewed his resume with an eye toward positioning his skills in the best possible way for the market. His skills were present, but not obvious. He also neglected to include some relevant experience, that of working in the family architecture firm creating technical documents, dismissing it with a wave of his hand. After our session, however, he decided to include it and many of the other suggestions found in this book. I reviewed his new resume and made some small suggestions, which he appreciated. I could actually feel his new confidence and wished him the best, not knowing if I would ever hear from Paul again.

One week later, I heard from Paul. He was hired for a contract to write a technical proposal for an architecture firm. They found his new resume online and were impressed with his qualifications. Paul sent me this email:

> *"I just wanted to let you know that I've just accepted a job as a proposal writer for an architecture firm. They called me last night after finding my resume on [Job board] and asked me to write a proposal for them. I delivered it this afternoon, they were impressed, and I'm already working on a proposal due next Tuesday...How's that for results for your resume and career strategy workshop! I didn't even have time to do the last round of editing."* —Paul

Paul's situation is common. No matter how qualified you are, you need to be packaged the right way to get your resume noticed. This book shows you the techniques you need to write effective resumes. These techniques are all part of the resume writing system.

In This Chapter

The topics discussed in this chapter are:

- Who Should Read This Book (page 3)
- How Will This Book Get Me a Job? (page 3)
- How Will This Book Get Me a Job? (page 3)
- Can't I Just Use Resume Writing Software? (page 4)

Who Should Read This Book

This book is written for online job seekers. Online job seekers are those people in any field who use the Internet to find and apply for jobs. Specifically, this book provides proven solutions for problems such as:

- Lack of experience
- Employment gaps
- Unemployment or underemployment
- Inadequate skills or education
- Competition in the market
- Poor response by prospective employers

If you think you need to be a professional writer to write a great resume, think again. You just need to be willing to do the work. This book presents the resume writing system in an easy, step-by-step way. Additional templates and resources are available at www.beatresumesystems.com.

A Book Designed for the Online Job Search

This book is designed for the online job search. If you look for jobs primarily online, then this book can help you.

For over 15 years, I have worked in the IT industry on teams that develop and implement IT systems, such as human resources systems.

Over the years, I've seen a lot of unemployed professionals who should have had jobs. Most of the time, their resume—not their skills—was the problem. They just didn't have access to the resume writing system presented in this book.

I developed this system by studying successful resume writing from all angles. I have presented the resume writing system to human resources staff, job recruiters (also called headhunters or agencies), and at several conferences and workshops. I have taught this system to hundreds of people.

I have many, many success stories that people have sent to me. Every time I receive one, I am absolutely overjoyed that another person has found a job.

How Will This Book Get Me a Job?

I believe you will get the best results—in anything in your life—if you first study and learn the system. Whether you are buying a car, choosing a university to attend, or getting a job, you need to learn the system.

Don't just learn one piece or one perspective. Do your own research. Learn many perspectives. Listen to many experts. Study the system like the future of your life depends on it, because it does.

I used this approach to create the resume writing system. I first created it for myself because, as a consultant who is continually hired for contracts, I was "always" looking for a job. I wanted and needed an efficient, reliable approach that got me jobs quickly.

When colleagues in my professional association noticed how well this system worked for me, they invited me to speak about it at workshops and conferences. I became the association's career and job coach. I taught the system to hundreds of people in these venues, as well as in one-on-one mentoring.

I learned even more about this "resume system" when I was hired to work on a human resources project for a global financial company. The project entailed implementing an online job system to manage the end-to-end hiring process, from the point at which candidates apply through to when they are hired.

This knowledge was invaluable. Over several months, I saw how these systems are configured in a variety of ways that are invisible to job candidates. These systems can be incredibly robust and picky. **If you don't know how to write your resume to expertly navigate through online job systems, then your resume may be deleted without anyone even knowing you applied.** Online job systems are discussed in more detail in "Tailor Your Resume to Beat Online Job Systems" on page 73.

As a professional writer, clients hire me as an expert to communicate messages and reach audiences. Since a great resume involves great writing, I loaded this book full of effective writing techniques you can use to create a professional resume.

How will this book get you a job? Every angle of the resume has been explored and presented in the way you need to navigate through online systems and come out on top.

Can't I Just Use Resume Writing Software?

I would love to tell you that all you need to do is buy resume writing software and you will have an amazing resume. The problem is, I can't. Resume writing software is just too generic.

Tip: Like generic resume books, resume writing software is geared toward the mass market, so it may be too generic to be useful.

In addition, the software may not even have your exact job title, so you must begin using a template that is not optimal for you. These templates may also include information that is just not suitable, since they are not customized for your region (how can they be when they are mass marketed?).

Possibly because of their need to appeal to the mass market, the templates included may look bland and boring. They are also designed primarily for print, not online viewing. If you primarily look for a job online, then you need a resume designed for online. For more information, refer to "Create Layout and Design" on page 13.

That being said, resume writing software can simplify your writing process and provide a structure you can build on. The software provides templates (or allows you to modify an existing resume), helps you organize your writing process, and provides keywords.

Example

Consider these phrases from resume writing software:

- Developed ideas for _____.
- Effective in stressful situations.
- Daily interfacing with engineers on various projects.

These phrases have some good beginnings, and now need to be enhanced. What were the results of the ideas? How does the ability to be effective in stressful situations provide value to employers (what did this ability enable you to do for previous employers)? What did interfacing with engineers accomplish? Simply listing what you did is not as important as what you accomplished and how you will contribute to future employers.

If You Choose to Use Resume Writing Software

People have used the techniques in this book to create professional resumes without resume writing software. If you choose to use resume writing software, then use it as a starting point. You still need to tailor your resume for the specific needs of prospective employers and online job systems as described in this book. Enhancing your resume is discussed extensively in "Boost Your Content (Good Secrets to Know)" on page 45 and "Tailor Your Resume to Beat Online Job Systems" on page 73.

Key Points

In this chapter, we learned:

- It's important to use a resume book specifically designed for the online job search.
- There are pros and cons of resume writing software.
- You *can* write your own resume, even if you're not a writer.

Next Steps

Now that you have learned how this book can help you, and that you can use this resume writing system successfully, let's learn more about the resume writing system in the next chapter.

Learn the System

2

Successful people know that success is a system.
Learn the resume system before you begin your resume
and you can succeed.

"I never knew there was a system to writing a resume. Now
I understand the right way to approach it."

Introduction

I worked with a top IT security professional who, in the best of times, was a millionaire. In fact, Mary told me her profession was so specialized there were very few people in the world who could do it, so she was always flying around the world implementing these security systems in financial institutions. Then, the recession began, and she was unable to find work for two years.

Mary may have lost her job due to the recession, but she remained unemployed due to her job search strategy. She completely dismissed the importance of a resume. When I pointed out that her resume was lacking in detail, and it wasn't readily apparent to an employer what she accomplished in these jobs, she looked at me like I had three ears, and said, "Any manager in my field would know. If I saw a resume with that kind of detail, I would throw it in the garbage."

Mary completely misunderstood the resume system. She didn't understand the related inputs, outputs, flow of information, and points of failure. Mary incorrectly assumed the IT manager would be the first person in the system flow to view her resume. This was a big mistake.

Often, it is the search engine of online job systems that you must please first, either in an online job board or a company's in-house applicant tracking system. If it doesn't get through this point in the system, it fails. You don't get a second chance.

TIp: It is the online job systems that you need to please first, not the hiring managers.

In fact, your resume may need to go through many stages in the online job systems before any person sees it. For example, when I worked for a top global computer company, resumes were not seen by anybody until they were processed for keywords, filtered, and ranked by their human resources system. As talented as Mary is, she may never have a job at a company like that until she changes her resume.

For your resume, you need to first understand the resume writing system *before* you begin writing your resume, not after. Using this system this way will drive the development of your resume in an effective way.

In This Chapter

The topics discussed in this chapter are:

- Resume Writing Is a System (page 9)
- Resumes Are Pivotal to Getting a Job (page 9)
- Know the Actual Purpose of a Resume (page 10)
- Think of Yourself As a Product Looking for a Buyer (page 10)
- You're Interviewed If You're Not Rejected (page 11)
- Impact of Online Job Systems (page 11)
- Influence of Social Media (page 11)

Resume Writing Is a System

As shown in the following figure and described in this book, the resume writing system is a comprehensive process-oriented system.

As a first step, learn the components of the system. The second step is to create an effective layout and design so you have a stable template. The third step is to boost your content with specific tips and techniques from this book, so that your resume is no longer the "plain vanilla" resume that thousands of other people have.

The fourth step is to tailor your resume for online job systems, and apply the techniques needed for your resume to be optimized in these systems. The fifth step is to keep your resume on top with more techniques that most people either do not know or don't do. Last, test and release your resume.

By writing your resume in this systematic way, you minimize the chances of rejection because you're meeting the needs of all the audiences (human and system) along the way. Time and time again, the resume writing system has shown itself to be a process that works.

Resumes Are Pivotal to Getting a Job

A resume is the single most important document you will ever prepare in getting a job. As such, learning the resume writing system is pivotal to getting a job.

The resume is a mandatory requirement of the hiring process. Most of the time, it is the employer's first impression of you and provides the basis for getting to the next steps. In interviews, it is the key document discussed to assess your suitability as a candidate. Lastly, it may be "finding you work" without you even knowing by being part of a candidate database.

Know the Actual Purpose of a Resume

The purpose of a resume is, quite simply, to get you the interview. Resumes are not your professional life condensed into a few pages. A resume is not a chronological history of every job you have had. For some of us, a resume like that would be 20 pages.

Jack Molisani, president of ProSpring Technical Staffing, says, "A resume is just a vehicle that shows you match what the reader is looking for—and that's all it is. If you know a resume is just a vehicle that shows you match what the reader is looking for (meaning, the job requirements), you can take steps to help the reader *find* that information and thus increase the number of interviews you receive."

So the question then becomes, how do you create a resume to enhance your chances at getting the interview? In the 30 seconds (some human resources professionals would even say six seconds) that employers spend looking at your resume, you need to stand out from everybody else. You need to be the one they choose. Over 100 proven techniques in this book will show you how to increase the number of interviews you are offered.

Think of Yourself As a Product Looking for a Buyer

The resume writing system has been developed with the recognition that you need to think of yourself as a product. You are a product looking for a specific buyer, and as Senior Recruiter Sup Das says, it's a buyer's market.

So, you need to understand who your buyers are and what they want and need. Present yourself in the way that matters most to hiring managers, recruiters, and online job systems.

Savvy advertisers know exactly who their buyers are, what they want, and what they need. Even though their ad may be seen by millions, they create their ad to reach their identified target audiences.

In the same way, you will learn in this book how to identify and reach your target audiences, and how to engage them. You can convince them that you are the right person to be interviewed by writing a resume that works.

Remember, there *is* a buyer for every product. If you are not getting the right buyers, then you need to be willing to change your product. Do companies release a product once, and if consumers don't buy it, throw it in the garbage? Of course not—they have invested too much money. They modify the product based on feedback from consumers, and then release it again.

Companies also re-examine their marketing strategy and find new opportunities for distribution. They aggressively market their products and believe in them. Companies inspire confidence in buyers that they have made the right decision by buying the product.

Tip: Companies believe in their products. Believe in your product, which is yourself.

You're Interviewed If You're Not Rejected

The resume writing system addresses the dynamics of resume rejection: how, why, and when resumes are rejected. Recruiter Jack Molisani advises that if you get an interview, it will not be because someone liked your resume—it will be because nobody rejected it yet.

You may be tossed into the reject pile because you have an unprofessional email address, somebody found a controversial statement you blogged, or your resume doesn't show what you can do for a prospective employer. This book provides top tips and techniques for keeping your resume out of the reject pile.

Tip: Your goal is to make sure your resume isn't rejected.

Impact of Online Job Systems

Obviously, a major part of the resume writing system is learning how to navigate through online job systems. These systems may be online job boards or applicant tracking systems (ATSs). ATSs are systems companies use for the end-to-end hiring process, from the point candidates apply to when they are hired. Most major human resources departments use online job systems to fill jobs. I was part of a team that implemented these systems and I have seen how they are configured. Understanding how to navigate through online job systems is critical to job success. For more information, refer to "Beating Online Job Systems—What You Need to Know" on page 79.

Influence of Social Media

More recently, social media has influenced the resume writing system. As social and work lives increasingly move online, prospective employers are right there along with you. More and more, prospective employers are using sites like LinkedIn, Twitter, and Facebook to find new candidates. The influence of social media is discussed in detail in "Tailor Your Resume to Beat Online Job Systems" on page 73.

Key Points

In this chapter, we learned:

- The resume writing system is comprehensive, and it needs to be.
- Your resume is the most important document you will ever write for a job.
- The purpose of a resume is to get you the interview.

Next Steps

Now that you have learned the major components of the resume writing system, let's learn the next step, creating the layout and design of your resume.

Create Layout and Design 3

If you want people to read your resume, then
pay attention to how you present the information.

Introduction

Dave owned a company that sold premium, top-quality exercise equipment. He decided his 14-year-old son would develop the company website as part of a class project. Dave did not want to find a professional web designer because he didn't see the value.

Dave didn't understand the need to pay somebody to make the content look "pretty" when he thought people really only wanted information about the quality of the product. He thought it was important to focus on the right words to advertise the product and its benefits, features, and specifications. People don't really care if it looks "pretty".

What Dave didn't realize is that looking "pretty" included creating logical headings to grab people's attention, placing information strategically so it pulls audiences into the site, and using appropriate (not irritating) colors.

Site traffic reports revealed that many people visited the site, but most did not go beyond the home page. They left quickly. How is this possible? He thought he had some of the best products on the market.

One of Dave's loyal customers who also abandoned the site upon accessing it called him and gave some friendly advice: "What does it say about your business that you can't present yourself professionally in every aspect? When I'm being bombarded to buy from every direction, if everybody appears similar I'm going to look at the one who grabs my attention first." Simply said, looks matter.

For your resume, incorporate smart layout and design principles so your resume is professional, and information is easy to find.

In This Chapter

The topics discussed in this chapter are:

Free Resume Templates Available

There are many decent resume templates and examples available online. There are even free resume builders and creators. These systems won't do all the work for you, but they will give you a base to build upon and modify according to the strategies in this and subsequent chapters.

To find free resume templates, search online for "resume templates", "resume builders", and "resume creators". Free resume templates are also available at www.beatresumesystems.com.

Important: Modify Templates for Your Industry

Whichever resume template you choose, be mindful that you may need to modify it to meet the information requirements of your specific job and industry. Examples of industries include accounting, automotive, banking, and information technology.

Learn how to modify the template by comparing it to resumes of people in your field and job posting requirements. For example, by reviewing IT job postings you would learn which computer skills figure prominently in IT job postings. You would learn that you must have a Computer and Technical Skills section, and that you should consider moving that section to near the top of your resume.

The majority of information in this chapter and the templates provided online are suitable for most industries.

Why Layout and Design Matters

There are definite reasons why layout and design matters in resumes, and these reasons have everything to do with your target audiences.

Suppose two resumes are sent to a hiring manager. The two candidates are generally equal, except that one resume has a better layout and design. It uses an online font so it is easier to read the text. The text is not crammed together and there is a lot of white space. Computer skills are categorized and easy to scan. Best of all, a Summary of Qualifications section details the candidate's best qualifications and is perfectly tailored toward the job. The information is so much easier to find in this resume.

After reviewing 100 resumes that day, the hiring manager's sore eyes just naturally gravitate toward the one that is more visually appealing. Not only is it easier to read, but it is impressive that the candidate has taken his audience into consideration—meaning the hiring manager himself, who is busy, fatigued, and wants to find information quickly. He conducted his regular scan and then read more of this candidate's resume because the candidate appeared to be a professional at first glance.

After the name, he reviewed the Summary of Qualifications section. Since the Summary of Qualifications section met his needs, he kept going to review other sections, such as the Education section and the Computer and Technical Skills section. Next, he checked for brand name companies, appropriate job titles, steady (but not short) employment, and multiple contracts. *At this point, he knows the resume is worth his time to read.*

In fact, Michael Spiro, president of Midas Recruiting, says *professionally written resumes seem to be more effective because of the formatting.* Resumes that do not have good layout and design just appear to be a big jumble of words with no path to follow (http://michaelspiro.wordpress.com).

Layout and design matters. Pay attention to the concepts in this chapter to learn how to structure your resume template effectively.

▶ Doing It Yourself

To create an effective layout and design for your resume:

- Use the free templates available at www.beatresumesystems.com.
- Use the concepts of layout and design in this chapter.

Easiest Way to Best Design

The easiest way to best layout and design is to read great resumes and notice patterns in resumes you like, as discussed in this section.

Read Good Resumes Before You Begin

There are a lot of resume-writing services that would be happy to charge you a lot of money, says Michael Spiro, but the easiest way to get a professional-looking resume is to copy somebody else's format.

Before you begin writing the first draft, make sure you read good resumes. Read resumes of people who have the job that you want and of people you respect. Search online for resumes in your field and pretend you are a human resources professional, scanning them to gauge which ones you like yourself.

Tip: Before you begin writing, read good resumes.

Why do you like one resume and not another? Notice what grabs your attention. Why would you interview this person? Why did you stop reading his resume? Why did you continue to read hers?

Also, visit the websites of resume writers and check out their samples. In particular, I would suggest that resume writers who have kept pace with social media such as Twitter are better suited to providing samples because they are more likely to have kept up-to-date with resume trends. Social media is discussed in detail in "Tailor Your Resume to Beat Online Job Systems" on page 73.

Notice Patterns in Resumes You Like

In resumes you like, notice what is the same. Notice what is different. Notice the patterns. Which keywords are similar? Which keywords should *you* have? Notice the key phrases, general format, special terminology, and layout and design. Make personal notes of your impressions and save them for your own resume.

▶ Doing It Yourself

To create the best design for your resume:

- Check out the resume samples of well-known resume writing experts, especially the ones who use social media, such as Twitter.
- Notice what you like and don't like about the resume samples you find.
- Use the free templates at www.beatresumesystems.com.

Problematic Design Elements

There are some problematic design elements that could cause your resume to be distorted or even rejected by online job systems. Avoid the following design problems.

Headers and Footers

Many online job systems can't process headers or footers properly. There is a risk that this information may not be read at all, so it's best to avoid them and place all information in the actual body of the document.

Columns, Tables, and Text Boxes

Many online job systems can't process information in columns, tables, or text boxes properly, so it's best to avoid them. Rather, to highlight and organize content, try variations in fonts, a moderate amount of color, blank lines, and generous white space.

Graphics

Avoid graphics. If desired, you can use relevant icons such as a telephone before a phone number or a logo such as LinkedIn.

✓ **Good Example: Graphics**

Debbie Prodder
Administration Assistant
☎ (555) 555-5555 ✉ debbie.prodder555@simpatico.ca
Linked🔲 *http://www.linkedin.com/in/debbieprodder*

Poor Text Alignment

If a resume seems difficult to read, or has a jumbled appearance, there may be alignment problems. Likely, there are too many instances of indented and/or centered text. Here is an example of poor text alignment, followed by an example of good text alignment.

⊘ **Poor Example: Text Alignment**

- Ten years of experience in senior administration roles delivering outstanding support to several federal departments, as evidenced by performance evaluations.
- Adept learner with strong adaptive skills to excel in a variety of environments, such as post-secondary, health, federal government, and education.
- Five years of experience applying complex federal government policy and communicating this information to internal and external audiences.
- Strive to develop productive relationships at all levels of the organization by using formal experience in education, psychology, and leadership.
- Excel in multiple-priority environments that have high standards of service.
- Fluency in English, Italian, and Spanish.
- Degrees in education, psychology, and history.

✓ **Good Example: Text Alignment**

- Ten years of experience in senior administration roles delivering outstanding support to several federal departments, as evidenced by performance evaluations.
- Adept learner with strong adaptive skills to excel in a variety of environments, such as post-secondary, health, federal government, and education.
- Five years of experience applying complex federal government policy and communicating this information to internal and external audiences.
- Strive to develop productive relationships at all levels of the organization by using formal experience in education, psychology, and leadership.
- Excel in multiple-priority environments that have high standards of service.
- Fluency in English, Italian, and Spanish.
- Degrees in education, psychology, and history.

Lack of White Space

"White space" refers to the blank space on a page. When resumes lack white space, they can appear overwhelming to look at. Use generous margins (about one inch on all sides) and space in between sections. Having generous margins will also allow for a shorter line length, which in usability studies have shown to ease eye fatigue.

Some job seekers' resumes lack white space because they are concerned about the length of their resume and cram the content on as few pages as possible. For more information about page length, refer to "Page Length—How Long Should It Be" on page 64.

Here is an example of poor use of white space, followed by a good example that makes the resume easier to read.

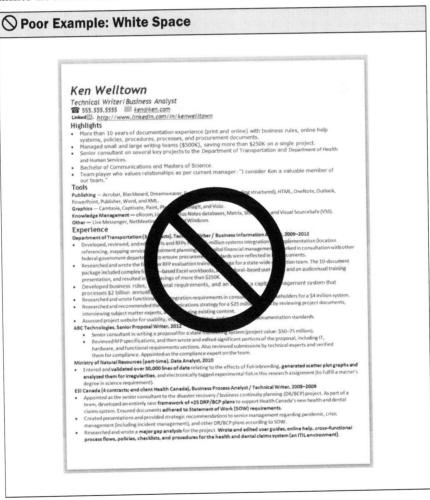

🚫 **Poor Example: White Space**

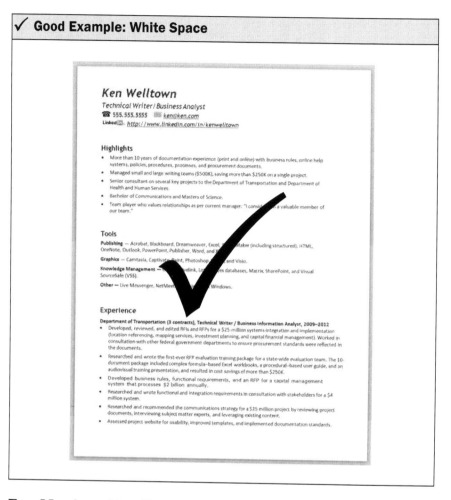

✓ **Good Example: White Space**

Too Much or Not Enough Color

Either too much or too little color can be a problem. A resume with only black and white text may be harsh to view online, so a splash of color in the headings (such as with dark blue) is a good technique to soften the online experience.

Inappropriate or Uncommon Fonts

Do not use inappropriate or uncommon fonts, as they may not be read by all systems. Also avoid using ALL CAPS, which is difficult to read, especially as body text.

As an online job seeker, your resume will be read almost exclusively online first, so use a common online font (called a sans serif font) to make your resume easier to read. Common online fonts include Arial and Verdana.

Online fonts are also easier to read in a smaller size than print fonts, so you can add more content per space than with a print font. (Personally, I like experimenting with fonts because the right font can reduce the size of resumes by a half page, for those size-conscious people.)

You can also use a different font for headings than body text. This will help separate headings from content and make it easier for readers to find content.

▶ Doing It Yourself

To avoid problematic design elements in your resume:

- Do not place important information in the headers or footers.
- Do not use columns, tables, or text boxes.
- Avoid most graphics, except small images, if appropriate.
- Use plenty of white space.
- Use an appropriate amount of color.
- Use an online font in most cases. Optionally, use a different font for headings to make separate sections more distinct.
- Avoid inappropriate or uncommon fonts. Some systems can't read them.
- Avoid using ALL CAPS because it is too difficult to read.
- Use the free templates available at www.beatresumesystems.com.

Use a Chronological Format

While there are a few common resume formats, the best resume format is called chronological (or reverse chronological), named so because it shows your professional experience in chronological order, beginning with the most recent position.

The most recent position generally contains the most information and the oldest position contains the least amount of information, like an inverted triangle, says Senior Recruiter Sup Das.

Here is a partial example of a resume in the chronological format. Notice how the jobs are listed in chronological order, beginning with the most recent one.

✓ **Good Example: Chronological Format**

Experience

2006-2012   Administrative Officer (multiple contract renewals), Solicitor General
- Researched and wrote executive correspondence according to departmental policies and procedures.
- Reviewed and edited documents for effectiveness of content, accuracy, format, and style prior to release.
- Planned meetings and special events for major federal initiatives.

2003-2006   Teaching Assistant, Elmvale Public School
- Selected appropriate instructional methods and learning materials for age and academic level of students.
- Effectively resolved behavior-related situations through the use of appropriate communication and conflict resolution techniques.
- Observed and evaluated student progress using a variety of assessment tools.

2001-2003   Research Assistant, University of Indiana
- Scheduled the studies and participants according to the needs of the study and the availability of the team.
- Transcribed personal information during the experiment in a manner that respected privacy and confidentiality.
- Created database files and maintained research information; retrieved and coded statistical data.
- Administered grant money and subject payments.

Why Employers Like a Chronological Format

The reason the chronological format is the best is because employers like it the most. It is easy for them to see when and where you gained your experience. Sup Das says employers also prefer this format because they weigh the most recent experience more heavily, and so this experience should be listed first.

Remember, the easier you make somebody's job and save them time, the more willing they are to work with you. The chronological format is also favored by online job systems because this format is easily processed.

Tip: Employers like the chronological resume format the best.

Pros and Cons of the Chronological Format

The chronological format works very well for people with a steady history of employment, especially where there has been progression. The experience is shown directly under the name of your employer, along with the dates of employment.

The chronological format presents challenges where there has been unemployment or stagnation, because these gaps become immediately obvious.

In these cases, some people use other resume formats, such as the functional format. The functional format separates your experience from where you gained it (for an example, search online for functional resume). To most hiring managers, this format is a tip-off that the candidate is trying to hide something, such as gaps or insufficient (or old) experience. There are better ways to deal with these issues, and these are discussed in "Common Problems and How to Fix Them" on page 53.

▶ Doing It Yourself

To use the best format for your resume:

- Whenever possible, use a chronological resume format because it is favored by online job systems and hiring managers.

- If you don't think a chronological format will work for you, first try all the techniques in this book before trying another format.

- Use the techniques throughout this book to enhance your content and fix any gaps you may have. Also refer to "Common Problems and How to Fix Them" on page 53.

Resume Section: Header

The first information you need on your resume is the Header section, which is your contact information.

Important Information to Include

Include at a minimum your first and last names, phone number (but definitely not your work number), and personal email address. You may also include your job title. Refer to the examples at www.beatresumesystems.com.

Pros and Cons of Including Your Address

Many resume writers recommend including your full address: street, unit number, and city. Hiring managers can see right away whether you live nearby. This is advantageous if you live close to the company. Unfortunately, if you don't live near the company, including your full address could backfire. It's possible that you are willing to do a long commute or relocate, or that you have a relative in that city you can stay with, but you might not be given the chance to express your flexibility.

Rejection by Address Alone

One recruiter I worked with outright rejected candidates based on their addresses. He didn't even bother contacting them if he saw an address that was further than an hour commute away. Most companies prefer local candidates.

Make Your Address Work for You, Not Against You

Whenever possible, remove any barrier to employers contacting you. If you post your resume on a job board, you really don't know who will be reading it (which is another reason you shouldn't include your full address).

Think about where you are willing to work, and present your address accordingly. If you live in a small town but are willing to commute into the big city, then omit your street address and use the name of the big city as your major geographical locator.

Alternatives to Including Your Address

Instead of including your address, consider just including your mobile phone number. If it is a local area code, then hiring managers will know you live locally and will not be concerned about your exact address.

If you are looking for a job in a different part of the country than where you currently live, then takes steps to appear to be locally located. For example, buy a mobile device or internet phone number with a local area code.

Your Phone Number, Not Your Employer's

Respect your current employer's place of business and do not include your work number on your resume. The message that you are sending hiring managers is that you use your place of business for personal gain. Similarly, you will use their place of business to do the same.

Use a Professional Email Address

An unprofessional email address gives the impression that you are immature or just weird, so don't use an email address that is cute, childish, or unprofessional. For more information, refer to "Leave Your Purple Hair at Home" on page 68 and "Fix Your Online Image" on page 86.

▶ Doing It Yourself

To create an effective Header section for your resume:

- At a minimum, include your full name, phone number, and personal email address. You may also include your job title.

- Exclude your full address unless you live close to the company.

- Optionally, include your city and province/state, or the major geographical center close to you (depending on your job goals).

- If you are looking for a job in a different part of the country than where you currently live, then consider obtaining a phone number with a local area code and a mail box (with mail forward options).

- Use a professional email address. For other tips in managing your online image better, refer to "Fix Your Online Image" on page 86.

Resume Section: Objective (Optional)

Objective sections provide prospective employers with your goal for employment. Objective sections are optional, as discussed in this section.

Important Information to Include

An example of an Objective section is:

- "To secure a position in X in which I may employ Y and Z."

- "To secure a position in quality assurance where I may use my skills in creating and executing test plans, designs, and scripts."

Why Objective Sections Are Optional

Personally, I'm not a fan of the Objective section. One reason I don't find the Objective section very useful is this information could easily be presented in the nearby Summary of Qualifications section (refer to "Resume Section: Summary of Qualifications" on page 27).

Some people defend Objective sections by saying, "I want the employer to know my ideal job." The problem is, "Hiring managers don't really care what *you* want. They want to know if you fit what *they* need," advises Karen Schaffer, resume book author.

When to Use an Objective Section

Some people may want to include an Objective section if they are making a career change and have a clear idea of where they want to go. An objective is useful in creating a "psychological response in an employer by getting him or her to immediately focus on where you're going with your career, rather than what you have (or have not) been" according to the job site Workopolis. You may find an Objective section useful in these situations.

Tip: Only use an objective statement if you have a clear idea of the exact job you want.

Alternatives to the Objective Section

You could replace the Objective section with a title underneath your name ("Quality Assurance Lead") and/or your top skills ("Test Plans, Designs, and Scripts").

✓ **Good Example: Alternative to the Objective Section**

Bob Jones
Quality Assurance Lead
☎ *310.555.5555*   *abob@tester.com*
http://www.linkedin.com/in/abobjones

▶ Doing It Yourself

To create an effective Objective section for your resume:

- Know that it is acceptable to omit the Objective section.
- If you must use an Objective section, then make sure it follows the preceding guidelines. Otherwise, use the recommended alternatives.

Resume Section: Career Summary (Optional)

A Career Summary section, also known as a Profile, is a short paragraph that provides an immediate snapshot of you. It is intended to prompt the audience to keep reading. The Career Summary section is optional, as described in this section.

Important Information to Include

A Career Summary section may include:

- Job positions you are qualified for, such as quality assurance manager.
- Top skills, for example, leading projects, managing people, and planning.
- Key reasons to hire you (which employer needs do you meet), such as having an innovative approach.

✓ **Good Example: Career Summary**

A Quality Assurance manager with 10 years of experience in developing and implementing test strategies and tools in complex environments, including financial, healthcare, and government. A top-rated resource recognized as an expert in creating QA departments for five organizations. Excel in multiple priority, deadline-driven environments.

Alternatives to the Career Summary Section

Similar to the Objective section, the Career Summary section could be absorbed into the nearby Summary of Qualifications section (refer to "Resume Section: Summary of Qualifications" on page 27). In a well-organized resume, the Career Summary section may not provide very much value.

If you choose to include a Career Summary section, then be sure to focus on your prospective employer's needs. What do they care most about? Look at the job posting for cues, as well as the company website. Search LinkedIn, especially your contacts, to find out more information about the job environment. Always think about what you can offer that sets you apart from other candidates. If the Career Summary section is not an interesting snapshot, then they may not keep reading.

▶ Doing It Yourself

To create an effective Career Summary section for your resume:

- Think of qualities employers value and how you can provide information to entice employers to be interested in you.
- Add the title of the job position you are applying for.
- Add your top skills.
- Add key reasons why this employer should hire you (why you are different from everybody else).
- Optionally, consider excluding the Career Summary section in favor of a different format. Refer to www.beatresumesystems.com.

Resume Section: Summary of Qualifications

The Summary of Qualifications section (also called Summary, Highlights or Selected Accomplishments) is a key section in your resume. It is a quick but complete snapshot of how you qualify for the position.

Tip: The importance of the Summary of Qualifications section to getting a job cannot be overemphasized.

Important Information to Include

You may include the following information in the Summary of Qualifications section:

- Job posting specifications—These are requirements from the job posting.
- Skills—Your top skills, especially if needed by the employer.
- Education and certifications—As specified by the job posting or is generally needed in your field.

- Values—Ones likely to be favored by the employer, such as innovation, teamwork, and productivity.
- Results—Your top results that will help solve problems for employers.
- Testimonials—Excerpts (even paraphrased) from letters of reference or testimonials from satisfied employers and clients (refer to "Hone Your References" on page 108).
- Awards (even employee awards), contract renewals, promotions, accomplishments, commendations, and additional information as applicable.

Tip: It is recommended to repeat information from other parts of your resume in the Summary of Qualifications section as needed according to the requirements of the job posting.

Why This Section Is Most Important

The Summary of Qualifications section is the most important section in your resume, simply because hiring managers tend to go here first.

This section allows hiring managers to immediately see your best qualifications and a summary of your skills. Since they may spend less than 30 seconds to form their initial impressions, you can be guaranteed this section will be part of that quick scan.

Tip: Prospective employers read the Summary of Qualifications section in detail, unlike most of your resume.

As the most important section of your resume, it is not the place to be shy. For more information, refer to "Problem: You Are Shy" on page 62.

Tailor the Summary of Qualifications Section to the Job

When writing the Summary of Qualifications section, think of your target audiences. Tailor this section as much as possible to match the job posting and the company website. List your best accomplishments from your previous jobs, even if you are repeating them from other parts of your resume.

If you know more information about the opportunity, such as the technology requirements, then provide as close a match as possible for your target audiences. Don't make them do any work in figuring out if you are the right candidate. Do all the work for them.

Tip: Write the Summary of Qualifications section as if it is your best sales pitch to the company for why they should hire you. Create as close a match as possible to the job posting, even if you are repeating information from other parts of your resume.

▶ Doing It Yourself

To create an effective Summary of Qualifications section for your resume:

- Review the job posting and company website.
- Match this section as closely as possible to what is important to the prospective employer.
- Include skills, environments, education, values, results, testimonials, awards, and experience.
- Repeat information from other parts of your resume in this section as needed according to the requirements of the job posting.

Resume Section: Computer and Technical Skills

In some resumes, such as for IT jobs, Computer and Technical Skills is a critical heading. It may also be called Technical Qualifications, Tools, or Skills. If this section is critical to the job posting, then consider moving it near the top of your resume.

The exception is if you are a senior manager who doesn't need to use the tools. Check the job posting. If the job posting doesn't specify the need to use tools, then don't include them or include this section near the end of your resume instead.

Tip: The Computer and Technical Skills section is critical in the IT field, unless you are a manager who doesn't use the tools.

Important Information to Include

Populate the Computer and Technical Skills section with as many skills as you can and as applicable for your job title (as long as they are still in use by prospective employers):

- Database applications
- Environments
- Hardware
- Industry standards (for example, ISO and Sarbanes-Oxley)
- Methodologies/tools
- Networking/protocols
- Operating systems
- Programming languages
- Publishing/documentation management
- Software applications
- Vendors

Get the Skills

To understand which skills you should have on your resume, check the job posting. Better yet, compare several job postings that have your job title to understand which skills are really valued. If you don't have the right skills, try to learn them through online courses and free software trial downloads. Sometimes it is also feasible to learn the open source (that is, free) version of the software. On your resume, make the connection between the open source tool alternative and the one required in job posting. For example, if Microsoft Project is required, include the following on your resume: OpenProj (open source alternative to Microsoft Project).

Organize Your Skills

Be sure to group your computer and technical skills experience by category, sorting each category alphabetically. Use the same format to ensure consistency. For example, if you are a project manager and know both Microsoft Project and Oracle Primavera, do not list one as Project and the other as Oracle Primavera. Showing your ability to pay attention to detail is just as important in resumes as on the job.

Poor Example: Organization of Skills
Computer and Technical Skills Adobe Photoshop and Visio; Macintosh and Windows; Microsoft Excel, Microsoft PowerPoint, and Microsoft Word

Good Example: Organization of Skills
Computer and Technical Skills **Graphics:** Adobe Photoshop and Microsoft Visio **Operating Systems:** Macintosh and Windows **Publishing:** Microsoft Excel, Microsoft PowerPoint, and Microsoft Word

List Skills Separately for Keyword Searches

To optimize your resume in online searches, list each skill (such as a software program) separately. For example, replace MS Office with Microsoft Excel, Microsoft Word, and so on. Listing each program as a separate term will increase your ranking in online job systems.

⊘ Poor Example: Separately Listed Keywords
Publishing: Microsoft Office

✓ **Good Example: Separately Listed Keywords**

Publishing: Microsoft Office (Excel, PowerPoint, and Word)

Verify Current Company and Tool Names

Verify the current names of companies and tools, and update them on your resume if they have changed, for example, through an acquisition. You don't want to look like you haven't kept pace with your industry just because of a recent name change. Not paying attention to these updates may also mean you won't show up very well in online searches.

When to Include Version Numbers

In general, avoid specifying the version or the release date of the software just in case the online job system or human eye arbitrarily decides the version you have is not sufficient.

If the actual version number is very important, then the prospective employer will specify the version number in the job posting. Note that if the employer specifically requests the version number and you don't provide it, then your resume may be rejected in favor of somebody who did.

Tip: For some employers, the version number is most important. Know your field.

When to Include Level of Experience

Similar to version numbers, avoid specifying your level of experience with the software (for example, intermediate), just in case it proves to be an arbitrary reason to reject you. If the level of experience is very important, then the prospective employer will ask when they contact you—don't offer it in your resume.

Of course, if the job posting specifies a level of experience needed (for example, expert) and you qualify, then make sure you emphasize your level of experience by including it in the Computer and Technical Skills section and in the Summary of Qualifications section.

▶ Doing It Yourself

To create an effective Computer and Technical Skills section for your resume:

- Include as many skills as you have (if not obsolete for your desired jobs).
- Group by category (or subcategories if needed) for operating systems, utilities, environments, software programs, and so on.
- List each skill separately—for example, list Microsoft Word, Microsoft Excel, and so on, not Microsoft Office.
- Verify current names of companies and tools.
- Generally avoid version numbers unless they are specified in the job posting.

- Do not list your level of experience with each item (unless the job posting insists on "expert" and you have it).

Resume Section: Experience

Where the Summary of Qualifications section can be thought of as the aroma that hooks your audience, the Experience section is the good food that keeps them interested in you.

Tip: Most of the work needed in your resume is in the Experience section.

Important Information to Include

The Experience section tells the hiring manager who you worked for, when, and what you did. At the most basic level this section includes:

- Job title
- Company worked for
- Dates of employment
- Major responsibilities and accomplishments

For an example Experience section, refer to www.beatresumesystems.com.

Why the Experience Section Needs Your Best Effort

The Experience section, or rather the effectiveness of it, can be the most important factor in deciding whether you are invited for the interview. Because it is such a crucial section, ways to boost its effectiveness are discussed throughout this book.

Tip: The Experience section can be the single determinant in getting you the interview. Senior Recruiter Sup Das suggests to always show in your Experience section how you created value for your employers.

In particular, pay attention to the tips in "Boost Your Content (Good Secrets to Know)" on page 45, "Tailor Your Resume to Beat Online Job Systems" on page 73, and "Keep Your Resume on Top (Ahead of the Pack)" on page 89.

Managing Job Titles—They Can Make or Break You

Sometimes job titles don't actually reflect what you did and are so vague, confusing, or company-specific they don't make sense to anybody outside the company. One popular joke about useless job titles involves the candidate who called himself a "cutlery sanitation engineer" instead of a "dishwasher".

Poor Job Titles Hurt Your Chances in Search Engines

If your job title is vague, confusing, or company-specific, then consider changing it. Inaccurate job titles will also hurt your ranking in online job systems. Online job systems tend to use job titles that are commonly used. For more information, refer to "Beating Online Job Systems—What You Need to Know" on page 79.

Recruiters Want to Know What You Did, Not What They Called You

"I don't care what your job title was. I want to know what you did," says Jack Molisani, president of ProSpring Technical Staffing. He says, "Member of Technical Staff, XYZ Company" tells him nothing about you and forces him to spend his valuable time reading more of your experience. He may get tired of looking for this information and reject your resume in favor of somebody who knows how to write for short attention spans.

Tip: Guidelines are more relaxed about using exact job titles. People want to know what you did, not what they called you.

Clarify Your Job Title As Needed

If you have a vague, confusing, or company-specific job title, then do your audience a favor and change it to a commonly used title that reflects your true responsibilities. At the least, add the common version of your job title. Be careful not to give yourself a better job title than is appropriate (refer to "Be Ethical" on page 100).

One candidate worked as a project manager but her job title was internal coordinator. Because of her given job title, she was overlooked for project manager jobs. Her resume didn't even show up in search results. When she began using the job title that reflected her true responsibilities, she began receiving calls for project manager jobs.

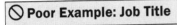

🚫 Poor Example: Job Title
Internal Coordinator

✓ Good Example: Job Title
Internal Coordinator/Project Manager

▶ Doing It Yourself

To create an effective Experience section for your resume:

- List when and where you gained your experience.

- For each job, include as appropriate:

  - Accomplishments, accolades (what coworkers or your boss said you did well), promotions, contract extensions/renewals, and awards.

  - Skills, responsibilities, major projects, special roles (especially if appointed), and committees you served on.

  - Projects and/or improvements you initiated and/or led.

  - Additional responsibilities you assumed.

- Context, such as special situations/issues that were a part of your environment or you resolved.
- Your results and productivity, especially if corroborated by statistics.
- Use your given job title if it reflects what you did.
- If needed, add another job title or use a different one that audiences can understand.

Resume Section: Education

The Education section contains formal and informal education. Normally, the Education section is found near the end of your resume. If the type of education you have is integral to the job posting, however, then emphasize it clearly, either moving this section near the top of your resume or repeating how you meet the requirement in your Summary of Qualifications section.

Important Information to Include

The Education section should contain both formal and informal education—this means college, university, certifications, continuing education, professional development, and any other courses that are relevant.

The format of this section varies depending on the job posting and your individual situation, as described in this section.

Creating an Effective Education Section

The information in the Education section is not static, meaning that you should consider adapting it to suit the job requirements, as per the guidance in this section.

Include Keywords That Matter

Keywords are important, so be sure to include courses (and descriptions of those courses) that would interest prospective employers. Refer to the keywords in job posting or on company websites.

If the name of the degree doesn't provide enough information about your qualifications, then be sure to provide a common sense name along with it. For example, a Bachelor of Science could mean you graduated from an IT or a biology program. Clarify as needed for your audience in a way that presents your qualifications in the best way.

⊘ Poor Example: Education Keywords
Education • Bachelor of Science, Bertrand University.

> ### ✓ Good Example: Education Keywords
>
> Education
> • Bachelor of Science (Health Sciences specialization), Bertrand University. Coursework in human physiology, clinical and laboratory standards, epidemiology, and radiology.

Include Your GPA (If Excellent)

You can also include your GPA (if it was excellent) or a text description such as summa cum laude. You worked hard for these grades and hiring managers recognize hard workers through their grades. Here is an example of how you can include your GPA.

> ### ✓ Good Example: Excellent GPA
>
> Bachelor of Science (Health Sciences, GPA 4.0), Bertrand University.

Take Continuing Education Courses

Continuing education is particularly important in some fields, such as technology. Courses you take online or from professional associations present you as a candidate who is dedicated to keeping current. It's not necessary to include all of them if it is a really long list, but do include ones that are relevant to the job position.

Use Education to Fill in Gaps

If you have a gap in your professional experience because you took time off to upgrade your education and skills, then consider adding education to your Experience section as well as your Education section, so the gap is accounted for. Your job title would be "student", and you would add the skills you learned and projects you worked on, especially if your deliverables were for an end client, such as the educational institution or corporate clients. For more information, refer to "Problem: You Have Gaps in the Experience Section" on page 55.

Here is an example of how education can be used to fill gaps in the Experience section:

> ### ✓ Good Example: Filling Gaps with Education
>
> 2008–2012   Student, Interactive Media, DePaul University College
> • Successfully completed a Bachelor of Science in interactive media. Designed and created websites, coded HTML, and conducted usability tests.

Omit Education Dates When Not Advantageous

If age is an issue—you believe you are either too young or too old—then omit the education dates. It is the easiest way for employers to calculate your approximate age. On the other hand, if you have returned to school to complete a degree later in life, you could include the date of your last degree to show how current you are. For more information, refer to "Problem: Your Dates Are Hurting You" on page 59.

Delete High School

Delete high school references from your resume. It doesn't help you appear professional when you are presenting your life as a teenager. If you graduated from high school less than five years ago and were a real star with outstanding accomplishments, an exception may be made.

Verify Accuracy

Always make sure you verify the correct name of the educational institution and the degree/certification. Avoid acronyms and abbreviations that may cause problems in keyword searches.

Education Problems and How to Fix Them

For one reason or another, there may be problems with your education. Perhaps you don't have college or university education, or you didn't complete it. Maybe you haven't been back to school in 20 years. This section provides guidance on how to fix issues with your education.

Problem: Didn't Complete Your Education

If you didn't complete your education, then try to present it as favorably as you can, and don't place this section at the top of your resume. In addition, give yourself credit for the number of years you did attend, as long as you do not provide any false impressions.

One candidate, who several years ago, completed three years of a four-year degree tentatively planned to finish her degree in a couple of years. She wasn't sure if she would be successful due to family obligations, but decided specifying an anticipated graduation date was the best way to present her unfinished education.

⃠ Poor Example: Uncompleted Education

- University of Waterloo. One year of Bachelor of Mathematics. 2008–2009.
- University of Toronto. Three years of Bachelor of Computer Science. 2009–2012.

✓ Good Example: Uncompleted Education

- Bachelor of Mathematics (one year). University of Waterloo. Courses in statistics, calculus, and informatics.
- Bachelor of Computer Science (anticipated graduation date 2014). University of Toronto.

Problem: Need a Degree, Not a Diploma

Some diplomas are actually equivalent to degrees. If this is the case, and you know that a degree is important to a prospective employer, then get the credit for it. Don't assume your audience will understand the degree equivalence and provide it for them.

⃠ Poor Example Presenting Degree Equivalence
• ABC College, Diploma of Computer Technology.

✓ Good Example: Presenting Degree Equivalence
• ABC College, Diploma of Computer Technology (Bachelor of Computer Science equivalence).

Problem: Do Not Have College Education

If you do not have any college education, then do not list your Education section near the top of your resume. Try to compensate the lack of education by emphasizing or pursuing continuing and informal education.

Problem: Not Enough Continuing and Informal Education

Be sure to include all the continuing and informal education that is relevant to the job posting. Some employers are willing to overlook the lack of college education if candidates show they are dedicated to learning and have the skills.

In some professions, it is acceptable to gain experience informally; however, we really don't want to hear that our surgeon gained his experience through discussion groups and by watching operations on YouTube. You can gain many skills through informal and self-directed education, such as learning software.

If the job posting specifically mentions that a degree is a requirement, then for this particular job, education will be a hurdle for you because of the ways resumes are filtered and ranked. In these cases, be sure to put your resume directly in front of people. Or, as one enterprising candidate did, build up such an outstanding consulting reputation and database of testimonials that nobody cared whether he had a degree.

Another creative IT professional who became an expert in his field obtained a part-time teaching position, despite his lack of education (which shows how amazing he is). For his Education section, he just listed his teaching position, "Instructor, ABC College" and all his certifications. Getting the job wasn't a hurdle for him.

▶ Doing It Yourself

To create an effective Education section for your resume:

- Include all education you have, formal and informal (if relevant).
- Add information about your degree, certifications, and coursework (if relevant). If the name of the degree is not well understood, then include an additional descriptor.
- Include grades or GPA, if excellent.
- If education is emphasized in the job posting, then show your education qualifications prominently.
- If you have a gap in your experience because you were a student, then include your education in two places: the Education section and the Experience section.
- Omit dates when education was obtained unless it's advantageous to you.
- Delete references to high school.
- Use the formal name of your education degree/certification and institution for effective keyword searches.
- Present your education in the way that shows you in the most favorable way:
  - If you didn't finish your degree, then include what you have.
  - If you don't have a degree but have equivalent education, then mention it.
  - If you don't have a degree at all, then take continuing and informal education courses, and list all that is relevant.

Optional Sections You May Include

Candidates often ask whether they can include other sections on their resumes. The answer is *maybe*. Since you are unique from every other candidate, there may be additional sections you would like to include.

Tip: Include optional sections if the job posting or your field warrants it.

List of Optional Sections

Optional sections you can add to your resume include:

- Affiliations or associations
- Awards and honors (for example, employee of the month)
- Hobbies
- Internships
- Languages (spoken and written)
- Military history
- Patents, including patents pending

- Presentations, teaching, and guest lecturing
- Travel experience, especially if the job involves travel or working in a global environment
- Publications
- Volunteer experience

Two of these headings, Hobbies and Volunteer Experience, are discussed in the following sections.

Hobbies

In general, do not include hobbies on your resume. Employers want to know what you do for them, not what you do for yourself. If your hobbies somehow enhance your application, however, then include them. The key is for your hobbies to be interesting or relevant. You may think your rock collection is fascinating, but most people won't. Use common sense.

Perhaps you volunteer at the same charity the company sponsors. Or you build computers for a hobby, and you're applying for an IT job (this was the case of a hospital orderly that was transitioning into the IT field).

Another candidate did some bullfighting when he was a young man. Although it was several years ago, it was an interesting hook that reeled people in. Who wouldn't want to meet a bullfighter who was now a business executive?

One candidate included his hobby of studying fish (ichthyology), and he proudly reported it prompted the hiring manager into talking with him. In this case, luck worked for him because the hiring manager had the same hobby.

Research the company (and the hiring managers, if you can) to find out if hobbies matter. Believe it or not, some bankers love ex-jocks. Use it if it helps you.

Volunteer Experience

Like hobbies, if the volunteer experience somehow enhances your application, such as showing you are a community leader, then include the experience. Otherwise, exclude it.

Always Consider How Perceptions Can Help or Hurt You

Always consider how volunteer experience can be misinterpreted and possibly send your resume to the reject pile. If you volunteered for a controversial organization, even when the perception of controversy was due to misinformation, then contemplate the pros and cons of including this experience.

⃠ Poor Example: Volunteer Experience
• President of the Cockroach Fan Club of Atlanta.

✓ Good Example: Volunteer Experience
• President of the Rotary Club of Atlanta.

How to Get the Best Mileage Out of Your Volunteer Experience

If you have volunteer experience that is a major asset to you, then you can elect to add this to your Experience section. Clarify the entry either in your resume or at the interview stage. Many professionals work for free when they generate new business, such as making cold calls and meeting prospective clients, but they do not downgrade their hard efforts as "volunteer experience" in their resume. It's part of doing business.

Tip: Show you value your volunteer experience by the way you present it, but be ethical at all times.

If you don't value your volunteer experience as genuine work experience, then nobody else will. Understandably, some employers will not share these views on volunteer experience. It is of utmost importance to be perceived as ethical at all times.

Example

Here is an example of how one business analyst who was unemployed decided to use volunteer experience for professional gain.

She was in between jobs and performed a significant amount of volunteer experience for her professional association. She wanted to get credit for this work, and rightly so, because it was high-profile experience. Notice how removing the word "volunteer" changed the image of the candidate.

⊘ Poor Example Getting Mileage Out of Volunteer Experience
Volunteer Director, International Association of Business Analysts, 2010–2012 • As volunteer director of programming for IABA, researched hot topics relevant to ever-evolving professional training of IABA members. In addition, secured reputable guest speakers to present on select topics that helped educate independent consultants. • As volunteer director of professional standards, directed, promoted, implemented, and measured IABA's ethics and advocacy plans for the local chapter. • Provided ongoing leadership and mentorship to junior members. Frequent guest speaker for IABA events.

> ✓ **Good Example: Getting Mileage Out of Volunteer Experience**
>
> Director, International Association of Business Analysts, 2010–2012
> - As director of programming for IABA, researched hot topics relevant to ever-evolving professional training of IABA members. In addition, secured reputable guest speakers to present on select topics that helped educate independent consultants.
> - As director of professional standards, directed, promoted, implemented, and measured IABA's ethics and advocacy plans for the local chapter.
> - Provided ongoing leadership and mentorship to junior members. Frequent guest speaker for IABA events.

▶ Doing It Yourself

To create effective optional sections in your resume:

- Avoid including hobbies, unless they enhance your application.

- Omit volunteer experience, except when it is relevant or advantageous.

- Add volunteer experience to your Experience section, if appropriate and relevant.

- Use other headings as appropriate for your resume. You are unique.

Popular Writing Technique to Show Your Best Stuff

A final word about layout and design for your resume. If you're having trouble digging out your experiences and qualifications, then use the writing technique of brain dumping. A brain dump is what it sounds like: you dump all the information about yourself onto paper or your screen. A brain dump consists of the following steps.

Dump Your Load

The first step in a brain dump is to dump your entire load. Do not be concerned at all with proper spelling and grammar. Do not be concerned about fine-tuning the details. If you have a brain cramp, don't get hung up about it. Come back later when the idea is ready to surface. Just write down all of your experience and skills as best you can.

Add to Your Load Over Time

The second step in a brain dump is to add to your load. When you do your brain dump, know that all the information may not come flooding forth in one session. Do what you can in one session and then populate it further in subsequent sessions. Capture ideas when they appear, otherwise you may not remember them later.

Get More Ideas

The third step in a brain dump is to get more ideas. Do not say "no" to any idea that comes into your head. Write it down in the brain dump. Show your brain dump to other people, especially those you have worked with, to add more details, results, and so on. Most people have a tendency to under examine themselves, so if you are like most people, you are missing some valuable information.

Revise

The fourth step in a brain dump is to revise. Writing is an iterative process. Very little is perfect the first time you write it. You make changes over several drafts until the content is complete.

Resume writing has elements of a creative process, because you are reaching deep into your mind to find facts about previous jobs and experience, and thinking creatively about how to transfer them to your current goals. Allow yourself the time to make these kinds of revisions. Be patient with yourself. Take breaks when you need to and come back to the task with a fresh mind.

Review for Accuracy

The last step in a brain dump is to review for accuracy. After you have emptied out your mind, and have ingested enough ideas from other people, review your brain dump with an eye for accuracy and detail. Fill in the gaps. Attach dates to experience, verify company and product legal names (as opposed to their common names), correct spelling and grammar, and so on. Any great tidbits that you don't need for your resume can be saved for the interview.

▶ Doing It Yourself

To get better information for your resume:

* Use the brain dump technique.
* Don't edit yourself when dumping. Let it all come out.
* Revise your content through several iterations.
* Keep information that you don't use in your resume for your interview.

Key Points

In this chapter, we learned:

* Looks matter, so have a smart and attractive layout and design.
* Ensure your resume doesn't use columns, tables, text boxes, excessive graphics, poor text alignment, inadequate white space, or too much or too little color.
* Preferably, use a reverse chronological format.

- Use online-friendly fonts, different ones for the body and headings.
- Ensure information is appropriate and strategic.

Next Steps

At this point, you have a solid resume framework that you can (and should) improve with techniques in subsequent chapters. Now let's learn how to boost your content, bringing your resume from good to great, so prospective employers are motivated to contact you for an interview.

Boost Your Content (Good Secrets to Know)

4

Use appealing words in your resume to really boost your content and make people interested in you. Words separate the good from the great.

Introduction

There were two shopkeepers who were brothers, Welton and Benjamin. They each owned a grocery store across the street from each other.

Welton's storefront was plain without any signage, except for the store hours and the "open" sign. Inside, his store was clean and organized. His produce was marked by plain signs, like his storefront: "apples", "oranges", and "bananas". He sold very good produce and was proud of that.

Welton always felt that customer loyalty and treating customers well was the way to do business. His customers who knew him already were pretty loyal, but he wasn't attracting any new customers, and as customers moved out of the area his business declined.

Like Welton, Benjamin treated his customers well but he also believed you always needed to "go get" your customers. Make life as easy as possible for them. Show them you are open for business. Tell them why they should buy from you: "10% discount means you save $3.30", "fresh locally grown apples", and "best produce anywhere within 100 miles".

Not surprisingly, Benjamin's grocery store attracted more people through his storefront. When they came inside, their good impressions were reinforced through more signage and good produce. It was easy to understand why Benjamin's customers would go there in the first place: he told them exactly how much money they saved, used descriptive phrases to help them understand more about his products, and really thought about what the customers wanted and needed.

Benjamin didn't leave the responsibility of understanding the benefits to the customer. He had the opinion that if customers did not come into his store, it was because they clearly didn't understand the benefits of doing so, and that was his responsibility, not theirs.

For your resume, boost your content with the tips in this chapter so people can easily see the benefits of working with you.

Tip: Candidates who make the extra effort in selling themselves through effective content are the ones who are noticed first.

In This Chapter

The topics discussed in this chapter are:

Choose the Right Words

Pay attention to the words you choose in your resume, since words are powerful. Words need to be appropriate and effective, as described in this section.

Use Proven Facts

Strive to use proven facts as opposed to subjective information such as your opinion. Including one or two personality traits or values in your Summary of Qualifications section is fine, as they indicate more about who you are and bring your resume to life, but otherwise just stick to the facts.

🚫 **Poor Example: Using Proven Facts**

• Intelligent and hardworking.

✓ **Good Example: Using Proven Facts**

• Bachelor of Arts. University of New York. GPA 4.0.

🚫 **Poor Example: Using Proven Facts**

• Works well on teams.

✓ **Good Example: Example: Using Proven Facts**

• Valued employee as per current manager, "Bill is a major contributor on projects and my team."

🚫 **Poor Example: Using Proven Facts**

• Provided superior in-class experiences to diverse and high-risk student populations.

✓ **Good Example: Using Proven Facts**

• Recognized by school board for providing superior in-class experiences to diverse and high-risk students. Assisted these students in improving their reading skills by one full grade within four months.

> ⊘ **Poor Example: Using Proven Facts**

- Significantly improved results of marketing campaigns by revising target markets.

> ✓ **Good Example: Using Proven Facts**

- Increased results of marketing campaigns by 25% through refining target markets.

Show, Don't Tell

It is much more powerful to "show" your skills rather than just "tell" people about them. For example, if you say, "I have excellent leadership skills", it is not as believable as demonstrating you do by mentioning leadership-related achievements. In fact, claiming you have skills that you do not demonstrate is not really believable. If people don't believe you, you have wasted valuable real estate on your resume.

Example

Here are examples that show the power of "show, not tell".

> ⊘ **Poor Example: Showing Your Skills**

- Responsible and reliable with excellent leadership skills.

> ✓ **Good Example: Showing Your Skills**

- Managed multiple teams for deadline-driven projects that succeeded in meeting every deadline.

> ⊘ **Poor Example: Showing Your Skills**

- Effective mentor.

> ✓ **Good Example: Showing Your Skills**

- Mentored junior help desk staff, identifying individual issues and building training plans with each team member specifically tailored to their needs.

Replace Weak and Vague Verbs

Weak and vague verbs—such as assisted, attended, and discussed—evoke weak thoughts about the person who wrote them. Replace weak and vague words.

Tip: For a list of strong verbs, refer to "Appendix A: Strong Verbs for Resumes" on page 119.

🚫 **Poor Example: Using Verbs**

- Attended status meeting and gave updates to management on issues and how to fix them.

✓ **Good Example: Using Verbs**

- Identified project risks and advised management on appropriate solutions to mitigate and/or resolve them.

🚫 **Poor Example: Using Verbs**

- Discussed ideas on best website design with clients and created designs.

✓ **Good Example: Using Verbs**

- Consulted with clients, and then created website designs that comprehensively met clients' specifications.

🚫 **Poor Example: Using Verbs**

- Worked closely with supervisor to prepare documentation packages for final printing.

✓ **Good Example: Using Verbs**

- Prepared documentation packages for printing according to company specifications.

🚫 **Poor Example: Using Verbs**

- Appointed to discuss company improvements with other employees.

✓ **Good Example: Using Verbs**

- Led the company process improvement group, recommendations of which were implemented by senior management to increase productivity.

Use the Correct Verb Tense

Use the current verb tense to describe activities in your current role, and use the past verb tense to describe activities in previous roles.

✓ Good Example: Verb Tense
Present tense (for a current role) • Develop requirements for construction software projects. Past tense (for a previous role) • Developed requirements for construction software projects.

Do Not Use "I"

Avoid using the personal pronoun "I" in a resume, however, "I" should be implied. This means that if you inserted an "I" at the beginning of the sentence and read it aloud, it would still read well.

⊘ Poor Example: Implying "I"
• Develops test plans for a global application.

✓ Good Example: Implying "I"
• Develop test plans for a global application.

Avoid Jargon, Acronyms, and Abbreviations

Jargon, acronyms, and abbreviations are some of the worst enemies of resumes. Jargon refers to vague, overused terms that are often used by one field or area of specialty. Jargon often leaves people wondering, "What did he say?"

Acronyms and abbreviations, if they are not in common use, may confuse your audience. Most people know what a DVD is, but does everybody in human resources know what PCN is? Better to spell out Program Change Notice instead (or at least the first time you use it). Alternately, use Program Change Notice (PCN) the first time, and then use PCN for subsequent instances. Check the job postings for cues on proper usage.

Tip: It's acceptable to use acronyms and jargon if they are standard to the company you are applying. When in doubt, spell it out.

⊘ Poor Example: Use of Jargons, Acronyms, and Abbreviations
• Harnessed key strengths of individuals to form a large global team for the ERDC project that developed and implemented a system release for FS.

✓ **Good Example: Use of Jargons, Acronyms, and Abbreviations**

- Managed a 20-person global team that developed and implemented a new release of the company's major financial system. The system was implemented in 10 countries and processes $2 billion annually.

How to Select the Right Words

Knowing you should select the right words is one thing. Knowing *how* to select the right words is another. Where do you find the right words and how do you know what they are?

The job posting provides the first cue. Read the job posting and populate your resume with as many of the keywords as possible, being careful to incorporate them into good writing as opposed to just a list. For more information, refer to "Optimize Your Resume for Online Job Systems" on page 80.

The second cue is found on the company website and through online searches. From this cue, you can ascertain the corporate culture and type of organization, including values, and modify your resume as appropriate.

As a general guideline (not rule), if the company you are applying to is an aggressive startup, focus on innovation, efficiency, and multitasking. If the company is a large organization, then focus more on process, policies, and quality. For more information, refer to "Know the Company Type" on page 77.

If you have written a generic resume and posted it on a job board (not to a specific company), then just write your best resume using the techniques in this book.

▶ Doing It Yourself

To choose the right words:

- Stick to the facts whenever possible, instead of your own opinions.
- Use the words of others to promote yourself.
- "Show, don't tell" your skills and qualifications.
- Don't assume that people understand what you mean.
- Take the time to provide detail.
- Use strong verbs. Weak verbs evoke weak thoughts about the person who wrote them.
- Never use "I" in a resume.
- Use the correct verb tense for present and past.
- Avoid jargon and acronyms, but well-known acronyms are acceptable (such as DVD). If you need to use a lesser-known acronym, then define it.
- Review the job posting, company website, and online news to learn which words have appeal.

- Incorporate appealing words into your resume as part of good writing (instead of just putting them in a list without context).
- For job boards, either use a more generic approach (use words that would appeal to the field) or use words that reflect exactly where you want to work (which company type).

Grab Your Audience and Keep Them

In this age of texting, we should all know that people have short attention spans and we need to make the information easy to find.

Write for Short Attention Spans

There is no question that you need to write for short attention spans. Even people who *should* read resumes, like hiring managers, don't. They are busy people who scan at a fast pace, so you need to place information where they will see it, or they may not even know it's on your resume.

Jack Molisani, president of ProSpring Technical Staffing, says he submitted a candidate who had the patent writing experience a hiring manager required, but the hiring manager promptly rejected the candidate. Why? As it turns out, the hiring manager didn't read that far into his resume. The candidate should have moved this information to the top of his resume. For more information on how to present information, refer to "Create Layout and Design" on page 13.

Tip: If your key information isn't easy to find, then your resume could be rejected.

Make Information Easy to Find

It's worth repeating: make information in your resume easy to find. If you don't, then hiring managers may not find it.

Give the same prominence to information that the job posting does. If the job posting emphasizes minimum education requirements, then repeat your education qualifications in your Summary of Qualifications section (since this is one of the first-read sections).

Jack Molisani contends that nobody reads your resume. People may scan it, read parts of it, or search for keywords. People just don't have the time. I agree with him.

Do the Math

Whenever possible, "do the math" for your audiences rather than let them figure out how much experience you have and where you gained it.

Tip: Add numbers and statistics whenever they present you more favorably. Examples include project size, money saved, or number of clients.

🚫 **Poor Example: Doing the Math**

• Several years of experience creating graphics.

✓ **Good Example: Doing the Math**

• Five years of experience creating graphics.

Appeal to Online Job Systems

Another key audience for resumes is online job systems. While you may not think of these systems as an audience, they are so vital that an entire chapter is dedicated to them. For more information, refer to "Tailor Your Resume to Beat Online Job Systems" on page 73.

▶ Doing It Yourself

To grab your audience and keep them:

• Write for short attention spans.

• Don't assume people read your resume—they don't.

• Put important information at the top of your resume.

• Make information relevant to your audiences easy to find.

• Repeat information if that means it's easier to find.

• Give the same prominence to information as in the job posting.

• Do the math for your audience whenever you can.

• Use numbers and statistics if they are positive for you.

Common Problems and How to Fix Them

Many common problems in resumes can be fixed by using the techniques in this section.

Problem: Your Resume Doesn't Match the Job Posting

If you do not use keywords from the job posting in your resume, then you minimize your chances of being selected. If you are posting your resume on a job board, then research job postings (about 50) and match those requirements.

You must "clearly demonstrate fit" advises Carrie Krueger, Vice President of Jobfully. You must also make your resume 100% relevant, leaving out information that might distract employers from seeing that you are a clear fit.

Apply the same emphasis to keywords in the job posting that employers do. If they emphasize quality control, and you do not include your quality control experience in the easiest and quickest way to find it (in the Summary of Qualifications and

Experience sections), then prospective employers may assume you do not have it. For more information, refer to "Tailor Your Resume to Beat Online Job Systems" on page 73.

Tip: Apply the same emphasis to keywords in the job posting that employers do.

Be careful not to add keywords haphazardly. As Carrie Krueger advises, "Don't cram your resume full of keywords leaving human audiences wondering why it lacks human touch."

At the end of the day, remember that somewhere along the line a human being will see your resume. You must be able to present yourself well.

Example

Here is an example of how using company keywords can boost a candidate's prospects to get a manager's job at a charity.

On a job posting, a charity stated that when you work for them, you're saying you care about children, their families and communities around the world.

Suppose one candidate called "Chainsaw Al" didn't bother to read this part of the job posting and believed he was going to be hired based solely on his qualifications, not the "fluffy" words his career coach wanted him to put in. Besides, in his job he wouldn't have any direct interactions with kids in an underdeveloped country, he reasoned.

The other candidate called "Smarter Guy" realized the importance of words and the perception they convey about a candidate. He knew that every person in the organization would be expected to embrace and reflect the company's mission statements.

The candidates were similarly qualified but presented their qualifications very differently:

⃠ Poor Example: Matching Job Posting Keywords
Chainsaw Al: Increased competitiveness through aggressive workforce reductions.

✓ Good Example: Matching Job Posting Keywords
Smarter Guy: Streamlined operations to reduce operational costs.

Look closely at these two examples. They both result in cost savings to the company, but too bad for Chainsaw Al. He won't even get a phone call from this charity. They can tell from reading his resume that he just doesn't fit their corporate culture.

Problem: You Have Gaps in the Experience Section

Many people have gaps on their resume, for one reason or another. Perhaps they stayed home to raise their children. Or they took time off work to go back to school. Or they had an illness. The fact is, a lot of people have gaps on their resume, and the truth is, they may not cause problems if they are presented properly.

Use Years, Not Months for Experience Dates

Sometimes gaps do not have to be evident at all. If you were unemployed since January and then started another job in December, then there would be no break in continuity if you used years (not months) on your resume. For more information, refer to "Problem: Your Dates Are Hurting You" on page 59.

Senior Recruiter Sup Das cautions that full disclosure is always the best strategy. If you are using this technique to hide information, then be aware that prospective employers are very astute about detecting misrepresentations. Be prepared to provide the full month and year as well as reasons for the gaps.

Plan to Fill in the Gaps

If you have gaps, then try to fill them if possible. If you know about a gap in advance, then you can plan in advance for ways to fill it. For example, if you are leaving work to have surgery, consider doing some self-study of new software while you are at home. You can participate in discussion groups, read ebooks, and view demos.

Here are some other ways to fill gaps:

- Tutor people in your field, even if for free.
- Volunteer (refer to "Volunteer Experience" on page 39).
- Take courses and certifications, even informal ones or self-study (refer to "Use Education to Fill in Gaps" on page 35).

Problem: You Stayed Too Long at One Company

A generation or two ago, working for one company your entire career was not uncommon. In fact, it was valued. You looked like a star. The perception was you were loyal and responsible, as well as a hard worker.

Now, unless you worked for a brand name company such as Microsoft or you showed progression and promotions, if you worked for the same company for several years it may draw suspicion. Can't she get a job anywhere else? Is he complacent or overspecialized? Doesn't she learn new skills?

Organize Information into Bite-Size Chunks

If you have worked for the same company for over 10 years, then it's likely you can fill an entire page with just one job. Since a page full of bullets is too hard to read (and we know that people don't like to read to begin with), reorganize your bullets into logical categories instead.

Example

Here is a poor example of how to display a long list of bulleted statements, followed by the good rewrite of how a long list of bullets can be reorganized into distinct categories to make it easier to read.

⊘ Poor Example: Organizing Information into Bite-Size Chunks

Quality Assurance Supervisor
ABC Widget Software, 2004–2013

- Actively fostered a quality culture by marketing the benefits of formal, well-structured quality assurance, quality control, and testing to senior management and other departments.
- Formally defined and established all quality assurance standards, processes and procedures (including the configuration and implementation of QA-related software tools and the creation of various templates) for the organization.
- Researched methods and tools that further increased the efficiency of the QA department—for instance, test automation reduced regression testing time by 50% when applied to projects.
- Identified and evaluated other departments' risks related to the Software Development Life Cycle and provided recommendations to the senior management team.
- Identified process improvement opportunities and developed solutions in conjunction with other department managers, including a metric-based code promotion process.
- Ensured pre-implementation reviews with project managers were conducted to facilitate smooth transitions into the production environment.
- Scoped, estimated, scheduled and resourced projects in negotiation with IT portfolio and project managers as well as senior management.
- Coordinated the efforts of project managers, business analysts, technical analysts, and software developers to accurately and efficiently capture the requirements of business clients.
- Identified project issues and risks, and then presented solutions to senior management and the steering committee.
- Researched and created various project management documents such as project outlines, project charters, business cases, and project plans.

✓ Good Example: Organizing Information into Bite-Size Chunks

Quality Assurance Supervisor
ABC Widget Software, 2004–2013

Quality Assurance
- Actively fostered a quality culture by marketing the benefits of formal, well-structured quality assurance, quality control, and testing to senior management and other departments.
- Formally defined and established all quality assurance standards, processes and procedures (including the configuration and implementation of QA-related software tools and the creation of various templates) for the organization.
- Researched methods and tools that further increased the efficiency of the QA department—for instance, test automation reduced regression testing time by 50% when applied to projects.

Quality Control
- Identified and evaluated other departments' risks related to the Software Development Life Cycle and provided recommendations to the senior management team.
- Identified process improvement opportunities and developed solutions in conjunction with other department managers, including a metric-based code promotion process.
- Ensured pre-implementation reviews with project managers were conducted to facilitate smooth transitions into the production environment.

Project Management/Staff Management
- Scoped, estimated, scheduled and resourced projects in negotiation with IT portfolio and project managers as well as senior management.
- Coordinated the efforts of project managers, business analysts, technical analysts, and software developers to accurately and efficiently capture the requirements of business clients.
- Identified project issues and risks, and then presented solutions to senior management and the steering committee.
- Researched and created various project management documents such as project outlines, project charters, business cases, and project plans.

Even though the candidate worked for one employer since 2004, organizing his experience into bite-size chunks demonstrated that his time there was well spent. This candidate was laid off from this position, and very soon after reorganizing his resume using the techniques in this book, he was called for several director-level interviews.

Tip: Think about the easiest way for your audience to find your information.

List Jobs in the Same Company Separately

If you have held multiple jobs in the same company, because you were promoted or just had a parallel move, then list these jobs separately under the same company. Detail the experience under each job so employers know these are separate jobs. The reason for doing this is quite simple: you want to show progression within the company, adding to the perception you are motivated.

In fast-paced fields, such as technology and telecommunications, working at the same company doing the same job for a long time could be perceived as a negative quality, not a positive one. The perception may be:

• You haven't kept pace with new technologies.

• You don't like to learn new skills.

• You haven't earned any opportunities.

• Don't let these negative perceptions get in front of the employer before you do.

Tip: If you stayed at a company for a long time, then try to show progression or increased responsibility by including new jobs or skills, parallel moves, or major projects.

Problem: You Have Too Much Unrelated Experience

At the outset, let it be known there is no "irrelevant" job experience. Every job where you have worked hard, produced results, given good service, and shown true dedication contributes to a positive impression of you. In addition, some skills are timeless to any job—for example, good written and verbal communication, creativity, and project management.

If you are entering a new field, you may have the challenge of presenting your previous job experience as relevant to new employers. In these cases, review the job postings and focus on your transferrable skills from previous employment.

Example

Here is an example of how unrelated experience can be transformed into related experience. Rob, a hospital orderly–turned–technical support analyst had a difficult time showing his transferable skills because he didn't know he had any.

Upon further probing into Rob's job responsibilities, he revealed that he had a considerable amount of general knowledge about medical procedures. In fact, when escorting patients to various labs, he would answer patients' questions himself because other employees were too busy.

Being able to communicate technical concepts to a general audience is a skill he would need in his role as an analyst. When users call the help desk with their computer problems, he would need to step them through the solution on the phone.

Rob realized he could present more details about his role as an orderly and these details would help in his search for a job as a technical support analyst, which focused on communication and technical knowledge.

⊘ **Poor Example: Transforming Unrelated Experience**

- Maintained excellent communication with a vast array of patients from different cultures, lifestyles, and ages.

✓ **Good Example: Transforming Unrelated Experience**

- Provided the first point of contact for patients undergoing medical procedures.
- Responded to patients' questions about medical terminology and procedures in a timely manner.
- Explained medical terminology and communicated medical steps in plain language, escalating to the next level of support as needed.

Problem: Your Dates Are Hurting You

Dates are precarious beasts. They can either help you or hurt you, but are rarely impartial.

Some candidates remove job experience older than 20 years so they do not appear "old". In fast-paced fields, such as information technology and telecommunications, the other reason to do this is that knowledge gained from jobs older than 20 years is considered too old to be of value. The exception may be if the older experience is somehow relevant to the job you are applying for and provides valuable keywords.

Other candidates omit the "month" in the dates of employment, just keeping the year, so that if they were unemployed for a few months it doesn't appear evident on their resumes. This is a preferred strategy, but be aware that you may be asked for those months during the prescreening or interview. Have your answer ready so you do not fumble.

Dates of graduation for formal education are good indicators of the approximate age of the candidate. Some candidates include dates of graduation so employers *can* guess how old they are, while other candidates omit dates for the oppose reason (they fear they are too old).

Even if you do not think you will be discriminated against because of your age, why risk it? After your resume leaves your hands and is posted online or distributed at a company, you can't be sure that everybody will share your point of view.

Tip: After your resume leaves your hands, you don't know who will read it, and you don't know how they think. Don't take risks.

Problem: You Don't Have Any Brand Name Companies

Hiring managers *love* brand name companies, such as those companies in the Fortune 500 list. The perception is these companies have better standards in hiring, so anybody who has a brand name company on their resume is automatically "branded" in a favorable way.

If you have not worked for a brand name company, then try to show you have some association with brand name companies, or at least a leading product. This is very advantageous for the online job search. Here are some tips:

- State certifications that are associated with a brand name company, for example, Microsoft Gold Certified Partner.

- State tools you use that are created by brand name companies, such as hardware or software programs. Even if you didn't work for those companies, you show experience with their products.

- Find something significant about your employers. Review the marketing material to get some ideas about how being associated with the company presents you in a favorable way.

- Associate the company you worked for with a brand name company, for example, "Project manager for ABC, an industry leader in mobile consulting (clients include Esso, Walmart, and Ford)."

- Be creative. One enterprising student of mine who didn't have enough brand name experience offered to review the course textbook I wrote for my class in project management. That way, she could include the job title of reviewer for a well-known educational institution on her resume.

- Get going. If you don't have any brand name connections, then start creating them. Can you help a well-known charity by creating a database for them? As soon as you complete it, you can add this accomplishment on your resume, regardless if they actually use the database.

Problem: You Are Labeled a "New Grad"

New graduates all have the same deficit: a *perception* of a lack of experience. This may or may not be true, but if you emphasize you are young rather than a professional who is looking for work, you are unintentionally contributing to this perception.

Tip: You can overcome the "new grad" deficit by recasting your experience in the eyes of a prospective employer.

Here are some tips to overcome the "new grad" stigma:

- Remove high school and high school activities, unless you were a "star" (refer to "Delete High School" on page 36).

- Place your professional experience before education, if you have good, relevant experience.

- Emphasize responsibility, independence, and results.

- Remove dates of graduation from college and/or university.
- Keep years (not months) in your Experience section so your summer jobs are not obvious.
- Make unrelated experience relevant to the job posting.

Example

Here is an example of a new grad who successfully reworked the negative "new grad" perception. While he did not have very much work experience, he contributed a significant amount of time to his community sports league coaching soccer.

To overcome the problem of a lack of experience, he emphasized the skills required for a job, including leadership, training, and communication. He started our resume session believing he didn't have very much to offer an employer, and walked away with several more value-added statements.

Problem: You Encounter Ageism

Another common problem is ageism. Ageism is the perception the candidate may be too old to be suitable for the job. Ageism does exist, so use techniques in your resume to reduce the risk you will be rejected because of ageism:

- Remove dates of graduation (refer to "Problem: Your Dates Are Hurting You" on page 59).
- Use a contemporary resume format. Refer to www.beatresumesystems.com.
- Use current keywords from job postings. Language is so dynamic that even paying attention to the subtle changes can rebrand you in a positive way.
- Remove obsolete tools and technologies from your resume if you know the employer is not likely to value them.
- Limit your experience to the past 20 years. Recruiters want to know what you have done recently, and experience older than 20 years is assumed to be obsolete. You may use phrases such as "more than 10 years' experience". For more information, refer to "Problem: Your Dates Are Hurting You" on page 59 and "Don't Write a Biography" on page 64.
- If you have worked for the same employer for a long time, then break up the experience to show progression, such as from one skill set to another or by project. For more information, refer to "Problem: You Stayed Too Long at One Company" on page 55.
- Create the impression you are up-to-date and eager to learn. Actively seek and list new skills, technologies, and continuing education courses.
- Use social media. Create a LinkedIn account and improve your online image. For more information, refer to "Fix Your Online Image" on page 86.

Problem: Your Resume Contains Discriminatory Information

Never give employers a reason to reject you. There could be many reasons why they would, and you want to avoid giving any cues about yourself they can use to discriminate against you. Avoid including the following information:

- Age
- Religion
- Marital status
- Political party affiliations
- Physical appearance (photos, height, or weight)
- Membership with controversial organizations

Rewrite potentially discriminatory information to keep the transferrable skills.

⃠ Poor Example: Combating Discrimination

- Updated and expanded contact lists of Labor Party donors, which resulted in a significant increase in party donations for the election campaign.

✓ Good Example: Combating Discrimination

- Updated and expanded contact lists of potential donors, which resulted in a significant increase in revenue.

Problem: You Are Shy

The worst place to be shy is in your resume. Many professionals are uncomfortable talking about themselves, but if you don't talk about yourself in your resume, who will? The next person in line, that's who.

Tip: To be successful, you need to be good at what you do and tell people about it.

You need to tell people about yourself in the way they need to know. Make it easy to find your "best stuff" and why to hire you in the Summary of Qualifications section. Also repeat that "best stuff" in the Experience section so hiring managers know where you earned it. Use words that show your work off. Also refer to "Value Yourself" on page 114.

⃠ Poor Example: Promoting Yourself

- Restructured the human resources department for efficiencies.

✓ Good Example: Promoting Yourself

- Restructured the human resources department, resulting in a 25% increase in process efficiency.

▶ Doing It Yourself

To identify common problems in your resume and fix them:

- Match the job posting keywords as much as possible, using the actual terms instead of synonyms.
- Review 50 job postings so you know that you are using the right keywords.
- Apply the same emphasis to keywords that employers do.
- Try to fill gaps whenever you can. The way you present gaps is more important than the gap itself, so be creative in filling gaps. Use volunteering, tutoring, education (formal and self-study), and sabbaticals.
- Fix issues with long-term employment for one company:
  - Present your experience in a way that showcases you most favorably.
  - Categorize your job responsibilities for easier reading.
  - List jobs in the same company separately, as this shows progression.
- Present your skills well:
  - Find out the skills you need from a survey of job postings.
  - Every job has relevant transferrable skills, so dig into the detail in your responsibilities to uncover transferrable skills.
  - Identify the timeless skills—for example, good written and verbal communication.
- Use dates wisely:
  - Delete experience older than 20 years unless it is very relevant or has valuable keywords.
  - Omit the "month" in your dates of employment (with caution).
  - Omit when you obtained your education.
- Associate yourself with brand name companies:
  - Know that hiring managers believe in brand names.
  - Transform your employers into brand names.
  - Volunteer, if necessary, to get brand names on your resume.
- Overcome the "new grad" perception:
  - If you are a new grad, then know the *perception* of inexperience is assigned to you.
  - Strive to create a professional perception of yourself to prospective employers.
- Deal with ageism:
  - Mitigate ageism by how you write your resume.
  - Use simple but effective ways to counter ageism.

- Combat discrimination:
  - Leave out personal identifiers, such as height, weight, and age.
  - Delete or reword experience affiliated with political or religious organizations.
- Promote yourself:
  - Don't be shy in your resume.
  - Make it easy to find your "best stuff".
  - Use words that show your work off. For a list of strong verbs, refer to "Appendix A: Strong Verbs for Resumes" on page 119.

Page Length—How Long Should It Be

The proper page length of a resume is debatable, depending on who you ask, but most people would agree it should not be a biography.

Page Length Debate

Number of pages is one of the most debated issues in resumes. Some career coaches say that a resume should not exceed two pages (one piece of paper). Others disagree, saying that resumes can be three pages, or as long as it takes to tell the right story. Senior Recruiter Sup Das says he likes resumes that are four to five pages.

A resume that is two pages may be appreciated by people who do not want to read, but think again about how this hurts your chances of getting hits. Remember, resumes are ranked in online job systems—the more keywords you have, the higher your ranking. For more information, refer to "Beating Online Job Systems—What You Need to Know" on page 79.

Tip: Cramming your resume onto two pages could hurt your chances in online job systems.

I agree that you should be very judicious in the use of space and not waste an audience's "eye time" with fluffy content or excessive detail if it is not needed (nobody wants to know you attended meetings). Don't delete great content and keywords, however, just to cram your resume onto two pages.

In all my time of writing resumes and giving workshops, only twice have I ever heard a hiring manager say he will delete a resume that is longer than two pages. In my opinion (which you are free to disagree with), it is a small risk to take when you consider the overwhelming advantages of having higher chances in online job systems.

Don't Write a Biography

Some people mistakenly believe they need to include every job they ever had in their resume. They ask, "Well, aren't I lying if I leave one of my jobs out?" No, you are not lying.

You are actually caring about your audience by thinking about what they are interested in reading. Nobody wants to know the summer jobs you had when you were 10 years old. Nobody wants to know every job you did since college if you are now 40 years old. Nobody wants to read about every single file you handled in your job.

If you include any job before 20 years ago, then you have to ask yourself *why*. In fast-paced industries especially, some 20-year-old technology is like digging up dinosaur bones.

At the same time, become familiar with the hiring process of the company where you want to work. Senior Recruiter Sup Das advises against deleting information without carefully considering the consequences. If candidates are subjected to background checks and it was found that some experience was omitted, this could appear as deliberate misrepresentation.

▶ Doing It Yourself

To determine the appropriate page length:

- Consider having three to five pages, and know that longer resumes are ranked better in online job systems.

- Do not delete great content from your resume just to reduce the page count.

- Don't write a biography.

- Tailor your resume toward the interests of your audience.

Be the Preferred Profile (Get a Good Impression)

There are a number of ways you can create a good impression with prospective employers through your resume.

Show Your Values

You might ask yourself, *what have values got to do with it?* Plenty. Values show what you will bring to the company and how you will contribute. Values show how you approach your work, and quite possibly what employers can expect from you in terms of teamwork, ethics, and productivity. After all, people like people who are like themselves. For more information, refer to "Be Like Them" on page 77.

Can you really tell values from a resume? Of course, you can't "see" how you work just by reading your resume, but you can create a good impression through the words you choose to describe yourself—it's in the details.

⊘ **Poor Example: Showing Your Values**

- Managed international website projects.

> ✓ **Good Example: Showing Your Values**
>
> • Managed international website projects, using cross-cultural awareness training to foster collaborative and productive team environments.

List Multiple Contract Renewals

If you have multiple contracts with the same company, then list them. Every recruiter will tell you that multiple contract renewals speak volumes about your performance. It shows employers, even before they meet you, how good you are.

Some candidates wonder whether they should save this gold nugget for the interview. The problem is, if your resume doesn't inspire enough confidence in the hiring manager to bring you in for an interview, you may not get the chance to talk about your fantastic repeat performances.

Tip: Contract renewals are like gold on your resume. Don't wait for the interview to talk about them, or you may not get the chance.

> ⃠ **Poor Example: Listing Contract Renewals**
>
> Marketing Assistant, Walmart, 2009–2012

> ✓ **Good Example: Listing Contract Renewals**
>
> Marketing Assistant, Walmart (5 contracts), 2009–2012

Mention Promotions

If you have been promoted or experienced parallel moves in a company, then mention these in your Experience section so employers can see how you have progressed. Mentioning promotions also shows prospective employers you are not stagnant, and are ready and eager to work hard. For more information, refer to "Problem: You Stayed Too Long at One Company" on page 55.

Be More Than a Brain

There are many very intelligent people who are unemployed. Being smart isn't enough. In addition to intelligence, you need people skills and a great personality. Check the job postings for skills and aptitudes you should demonstrate in your resume.

Some typical skills and aptitudes for jobs include:

• Ability to be flexible and manage changing priorities

• Ability to meet deadlines

• Ability to work in a high-pressure environment

• Analytical

• Continuous learner

- Detail oriented
- Ethics and integrity
- Excellent verbal and written communication skills
- Organized
- Problem solver
- Project management knowledge
- Self-motivated
- Team player

Generate your own list of keywords from job postings and company websites, and then think about how you meet those expectations. By gauging the kind of a company it is and profiles they prefer, you can demonstrate those qualities in your resume (refer to "Know the Company Type" on page 77).

Tip: Use the technique of "show, don't tell" to present these favored terms. For more information, refer to "Show, Don't Tell" on page 48.

Learn Project Management

Project management skills are one of those all-around important skills that prospective employers like, or even love. Even if you do not manage projects or people, everybody is responsible for managing their own work. I have taught a college-level project management course for several years, and the one comment that keeps coming back from my former students is how much the course has helped them manage their own work.

Tip: Many employers want you to have project management skills, even when you don't manage anything except your own work.

No matter how small the projects, every project must be scoped out and estimated. You also need to be able to manage change, mitigate problems, and meet deadlines.

Even if you never plan to manage projects and people, learning project management skills and showing them on your resume is a real asset because hiring managers know you are likely to be more efficient, productive, and process oriented than candidates who lack these skills.

Luckily, there is no shortage of free information, courses, and books to learn project management. Start with Google Books, ebooks, LinkedIn groups, and the Project Management Institute, the world's leading professional organization for project management.

Be Results-Oriented

Show the results of your efforts by using results-oriented descriptions. Spend some time to figure out the results you achieved for each employer. It should be explicitly clear what you did for them. Perhaps you met all deadlines. Maybe you initiated a process improvement that improved quality, or perhaps you fostered good relationships with clients, which resulted in additional revenues.

Tip: Senior Recruiter Sup Das says, "A great resume starts with great past performance."

 Poor Example: Showing Results

- Increased product sales by revising sales and marketing strategies at all levels in the company.

 Good Example: Showing Results

- Increased product sales by 15% within one quarter by revising sales and marketing strategies at all levels in the company.

Leave Your Purple Hair at Home

When searching for a job, be mainstream even when you're not. Even in a casual office culture, this doesn't mean that "anything goes".

While employers accept the stereotypical computer geek, they do not accept people who fall outside the range of professional corporate culture or mainstream society. The same goes for your resume: nothing cute, childish, or unprofessional. Only bring your purple hair to work if your boss does. For more information, refer to "Fix Your Online Image" on page 86.

Look Like the Locals

Too many qualified candidates ruin their chances for employment by not paying attention to local resume writing trends. This is very unfortunate. By not knowing what these trends are, qualified candidates don't have a chance. They are eliminated from the competition before it begins.

If you use foreign phrases or unclear English in your resume, other people may question how well you can communicate with your colleagues. If English is not your first language, then consider having someone who is fluent in English edit your resume.

Or, if you are applying for a job in a region where they use a different style of English, consider having a local person review your resume.

Tip: Take the extra time to localize your resume. If you don't, you may be quickly rejected.

To appear more like a local, rather than have your country's official name for your degree (which an English speaker may not be able to understand), include the translated name of your degree. Make sure the translation is similar to an existing local program.

In addition, if you worked in another country but actually reported to a U.S. boss, then consider omitting the reference to where you were located. With global companies and their mobile work forces, it doesn't really matter where you were physically located.

Make sure your resume is not eliminated because of:

- Foreign phrases and cultural different language.
- Ineffective page length (refer to "Page Length—How Long Should It Be" on page 64).
- Personal information, such as age, weight, and photo (refer to "Problem: Your Resume Contains Discriminatory Information" on page 62).
- Different values (refer to "Show Your Values" on page 65).

▶ Doing It Yourself

To be the preferred profile:

- Show your values:
  - Show your values, such as teamwork, ethics, and productivity.
  - Make sure your values align with the company or industry values.
  - Understand that hiring managers form impressions of your values by the words you choose.
- List multiple contracts and promotions:
  - List all your contract renewals.
  - Mention promotions on your resume.
  - Mention parallel moves or a change in responsibilities to show progression.
- Be more than a brain:
  - Find out the skills hiring managers want, and then prove you have these skills by "showing, not telling".
  - Learn project management. Hiring managers like candidates with project management skills, even if they only manage their own work.
- Create a good impression:
  - Use results-oriented statements. Whenever possible, find a result in the work that you do.
  - Err on the side of conservative. If your grandma wouldn't like it, then don't do it.
  - People will assume you have communication problems if your resume is written in poor English.
  - Pay attention to local resume trends.
  - Avoid foreign phrases, job titles, and locations.

Common Sense Points Worth Saying

This section describes some points that are common sense but nonetheless, worth saying.

Follow the Employer's Instructions

One of the easiest ways to get your resume thrown into the "reject pile" is to ignore the employer's instructions. One hiring manager told me that if the candidates can't follow basic instructions for how they should apply, he will reject them outright. Provide a resume in the requested format (for example, .docx or .pdf), using the requested naming convention if stated.

Check Spelling and Grammar

If you think that spelling and grammar do not matter because you're not applying for a job as a writer, think again. When your resume has correct spelling and grammar, it is like you are telling hiring managers that you care about detail, and doing every job the right way.

Tip: Make sure you check your resume for spelling and grammar.

Recruiter Jack Molisani concurs that even engineers need to be careful of spelling and grammar. He recalls what an engineering manager said about a programmer with typos in his resume: "If he can't write two pages of an error-free resume, how can I expect him to write 10,000 lines of error-free code?"

▶ Doing It Yourself

To do the common sense tasks:

- Always follow the employer's instructions, or you could be rejected.
- Check spelling and grammar. Regardless of your job position, your resume needs to be error-free.

Key Points

In this chapter, we learned:

- Words are powerful and can really change how employers perceive you.
- Audiences need to be "grabbed" in ways that appeal to them.
- Common resume problems can be overcome through effective techniques.
- Page lengths can vary but do not write a biography.
- The best strategy is to become the preferred profile, so match your resume to the job posting.

Next Steps

Your resume is almost complete. It is, at this point, almost ready to be released to employers. It could be even better. Let's learn how to further enhance your resume to move it to the top.

Tailor Your Resume to Beat Online Job Systems 5

To beat online job systems, you need to find out the
requirements of your target audiences.
Listen to them. They matter.

"It's not really what I was thinking about when I
mentioned a vehicle that was small and red."

Introduction

Good car salespeople know that if they don't listen to their audiences, then they
won't get the sale. In your resume, you need to find out what online job systems
favor. Since these parameters are driven by human resources (HR) requirements,
you also need to find out what the employer is looking for. If you don't listen—
really listen—to what they want or need, then you will be quickly rejected.

Angela didn't really think she had to work that hard to please anybody through her
resume, especially an online job system. She didn't bother with all the latest
keywords in the job postings. Nor did she bother with visiting company websites

and inserting keywords and statements that would appeal to the company type (refer to "Know the Company Type" on page 77). Angela didn't think these techniques would help sell herself.

"I mean, if I'm what they want, I'll get the job, right? Words from a job posting don't matter if I have what they are looking for. That's a lot of work to do, anyway, and I need to spend my time finding a job."

Now at that point, I had to stop Angela. "You need to find a job, yet you are not working very hard to appeal to your audiences—the very people who can give you a job. Do you know how many people have successfully repackaged themselves just by listening to what other people want?"

Online job systems are very unforgiving to people who do not try to appeal to them. They just automatically reject you. In my experience, HR employees tend to be congenial people, but they are overworked and understaffed, and may reject resumes if information is not well presented (even if you are actually qualified).

Take the time to find out what your audiences need and see your resume rise to the top.

In This Chapter

The topics discussed in this chapter are:

Your Resume Is Not About You

Your resume is not about you. Your resume is about your target audiences. Your target audiences include the people or systems you need to pass in order to get the interview. Target audiences can include anybody who can get you closer to the interview, including assistants, recruiters, managers and HR employees. It also includes online job systems, such as job boards and applicant tracking systems.

It is understandable for the person who is writing a resume to ask, "What do I want people to know about me?" but the question you should actually be asking is, "What does the audience want to know about me?" says author Karen Schaffer.

The more that you are able to show you fit your audience's needs and wants (in other words, the more you can resonate with them), the higher your chances are of getting the interview.

Online job systems are configured according to the requirements of the job. These requirements are driven by hiring managers and HR employees. You need to show—within seconds—how you match what the employer is looking for.

Tip: Your resume is about them, not you. Find out what they need and want, and then give it to them.

Example

Here is an example of why finding out what target audiences need matters. One candidate worked in the banking industry as an analyst using a near- obsolete system. She considered deleting the system from her resume because she wanted to appear more modern. After inquiring about other financial environments, however, she learned this system is still in widespread use throughout the industry. She decided to leave this near-obsolete system on her resume, realizing it actually gave her an edge over other candidates.

Care About Other People's Problems

When you write your resume and have the mindset of thinking about others, you automatically write a better resume. When you are able to step into somebody else's world and understand their concerns, issues, and struggles, your resume will speak louder to them than anybody else's. Senior Recruiter Sup Das says you need to answer the question, "What keeps them up at night?"

If there was no problem, then there would be no need for the job. Your task is to find out what the specific problem is, and then be the best candidate to solve it.

Tip: Caring about other people's problems will propel your resume to the top.

Example

Here is an example of why it matters to care about other people's problems. Suppose an acquaintance of yours told you that the primary struggle of the hiring manager are employees who can't keep pace with the aggressive environment.

You write in your Summary of Qualifications section (where the manager can easily read it):

"…met all deadlines in aggressive project environments…"

If you include that information, then your resume will resonate with the hiring manager. Why? They see somebody who can solve their problem. They see somebody who has *already* solved their problem. Also refer to "Know the Company Type" on page 77.

Techniques to Find Out What Target Audiences Want

How do you learn what your target audiences want? Just one word: *ask*. You can learn what your audiences want from:

- People in the job: Contact people already doing the job that you want to do. You can find them through professional conferences, associations, LinkedIn, blogs, and discussion groups.

- Search engines: Enter your job title into an online job board. Refine your search to information you are looking for.

- Hiring managers and HR employees: Contact them and ask them pertinent questions. What types of candidates are preferred (skills, experience, and personalities)? If you're too shy to be this direct, then take the online route and ask questions through blogs and discussion groups.

Do not anticipate that everybody will talk with you or be forthcoming. Some employees may be legally bound not to divulge details about their hiring practices, so just find other people to talk to.

Tip: There is an incredible amount of information available online. Be sure to verify it with live feedback as needs vary across geographical and industry boundaries.

Know Why the Job Is Available

How does it help you to know why the job is available before you submit your resume? By knowing the employer's needs and wants, and addressing them as early as possible at the resume submission stage, you are creating an edge for yourself over the competition.

Example

Here is an example of how knowing why the job is available can serve as an advantage.

A project manager position became available at a small engineering company. When the candidate inquired about why the position was available and what the environment was like, she was told that it was a small company (about 50 employees) that developed extremely technical survey equipment. The job was available because the manager was going on leave for six months.

The team she managed consisted of three employees who were all relatively new. Knowing this information, the candidate knew the company probably valued teamwork. She also correctly surmised that, because the manager would be returning from leave in six months, she wanted somebody to "keep everything going" as opposed to broad, new changes.

Essentially, she wanted to return to the department in the same shape and direction she left it. Somebody who would support her wishes was important to the current project manager, as she would not want to return to a vastly different department.

The candidate tailored her resume to the project manager's needs. She inserted phrases to show that she valued teamwork, worked well in small-team environments, was a supportive leader, and could manage a department within established standards. She did this again in the interview and was offered the contract.

Be Like Them

You need to show enough of yourself in your resume, including your personality, to let hiring managers know who you are. The more they know you, and know you to be like them—having compatible values, experience, and approach—the more comfortable they feel about you, even before they meet you.

In this business, feelings matter. You can argue that feelings should not be a part of business, but the fact is, people like people who are like themselves, and the more you provide hiring managers with that confidence, the more at ease they will feel around you.

Hiring managers want to know you will fit into their environment, know and understand why their issues are important to them, have an approach that fits with their sensibilities, and can solve problems they are having. They want to know you have the same values they do about the job. For more information, refer to "Show Your Values" on page 65.

Tip: Some candidates' resumes are tailored so well to their audiences that the decision to hire them has already been made before meeting them.

Know the Company Type

Know the type of company you are applying to, so you can resonate with them in appropriate ways. At opposite ends of the spectrum are small, startup companies versus large companies and institutions.

Small startups favor candidates who can work in fast-paced, multiple-priority environments where change is the norm. Small companies are more likely to have undefined processes, streamlined approval processes, multiple and shifting priorities, combined job roles, and more flexibility.

Large companies and institutions such as government favor candidates who can work in multistakeholder, process-oriented environments. Large companies and institutions are more likely to have rigorous documented processes (such as for change management), multiple levels of formal approvals, project management offices, defined job descriptions, communication challenges, and hierarchical decision making.

Of course, there may be some companies that are a bit of both. For example, a new pharmaceutical company would be undergoing a lot of change but at the same time is required to follow strict procedures regarding quality. Or, a large software company could behave like a small company in its decision making as part of a dedicated direction.

How does knowing the company type affect your resume? Qualified candidates have been overlooked just because it appeared that the candidate wouldn't fit into the company environment.

One candidate who interviewed at a large government institution was not offered the job because he had a lot of short contracts with private sector companies on his resume. The hiring manager believed that the candidate would not be able to adjust to the culture of a large government institution: regular hours, process, bureaucracy, and hierarchical authority.

▶ Doing It Yourself

To make sure your resume is not about you:

- Tailor your resume for your audience.
- Find out the problems hiring managers face, and then address their problems in your resume.
- Be thorough in finding out the wants and needs of hiring managers, as this can give you a real edge over other candidates.
- Whenever possible, inquire about why the job is available.
- Know that people like people who are like themselves.
- Show that your values, experience, and approach are compatible with the hiring managers and company.
- Be aware that feelings matter even if they shouldn't, so evoke positive feelings from others through the words you choose in your resume.
- Understand the type of company you are applying to—for example, know how to appeal to small startups versus large companies and institutions.

Beating Online Job Systems—What You Need to Know

Online job systems include both Applicant Tracking Systems (ATS) and online job boards, such as Monster. ATSs are systems HR departments use to post jobs and receive applications. They are end-to-end solutions that can be used from the point at which candidates apply for the job through to the letter of offer. They can track correspondence and documents.

Working on the team that implemented an ATS for a global financial auditing company gave me an entirely different view on how to write resumes. I saw how qualified candidates could get rejected just because they didn't optimize their resumes for online searching. The problem is, they wouldn't necessarily know how to do that, either, which is why it is discussed in this book.

Online job boards, where candidates post their resumes for viewing or apply to any number of posted positions, are another type of online job system. When companies post jobs on job boards, they can link directly to the company's own ATS. The strategies in this section apply to both types of systems.

Methods of Searching Resumes

ATSs search resumes in any way the companies configure them. Resumes can be searched by:

- Keywords: Keywords included in the job posting, such as skills, certifications, degrees, technologies, software, company name, corporate values, and industry keywords. Keywords not in the job posting, such as competitors' names, may also be included in the search criteria.

- Job titles: The exact job title used in the job posting, and possibly synonyms of the job title. For example, if the job title is "help desk agent" and synonyms are allowed, then resumes that include "technical support analyst" will also be returned in the search results.

- Date job title was held: The date the candidate held the job title, including "current", "immediate past", or at some other point in the past x years, where x can be any number of years. Typically, x may be within the past five years, which may be narrowed to one year if too many resumes are received.

- Percentage resume matches the job posting: Related to keywords, the more a resume matches the job posting, the greater chance it will be returned in the search results. Matching percentages can be specified—for example, if 50% is desired, then 50% of the resume content must match the job posting in order to be returned in the search results.

- Method candidate applied to the job: The job board the candidate used to apply for the job. The company can restrict search results to only those candidates who applied directly to the company. It is perceived these candidates have been actively visiting that company's career page, thus implying they are interested in working for that company specifically. Companies may also have online job boards they favor.

- Synonyms: Allowing synonyms for keywords in the job posting. If synonyms are allowed, then more resumes are returned in the search results. If too many resumes are returned, then synonyms may be disallowed.

HR employees can set basic criteria for receiving resumes, and then apply filtering criteria if too many resumes are received. For example, if 1000 resumes are received that include the desired job title, then HR employees can narrow the search to candidates who have had the job title in the past year. Or, if not enough resumes are received HR employees can expand the search to include synonyms for job titles. For more information about job titles, refer to "Managing Job Titles—They Can Make or Break You" on page 32.

Optimize Your Resume for Online Job Systems

Based on the myriad of ways that HR employees can use online job systems to search for resumes, the best way to increase your ranking in these systems is to:

- Match the job posting as closely as possible. Use as many of the keywords in the job posting as possible. It would also be useful to review the company's website and insert keywords related to their corporate culture and industry.

  Tip: Apply the same emphasis to the keywords in the job posting that employers do.

- Use the exact words, as opposed to synonyms or closely related phrases. For example, if the job posting is for a "technical writer", and your resume states you have worked as a "documentation specialist", your resume may not be as highly ranked as the person who has the job title of "technical writer". While these systems can be configured to search for exact titles and/or synonyms, HR employees may need to limit the search results due to the excessive number of candidates, and searching by exact job title may be one of the limiting criteria.

- Increase the number of instances of the important keywords. In addition to including the exact keywords from the job posting, the more instances you have of the keywords, the higher your ranking. So, if a mandatory requirement is "Microsoft Word", then find multiple ways to insert this term on your resume, such as listing it in your Summary of Qualifications, Experience, and Computer and Technical Skills sections.

  Tip: The more keywords you have, the higher your ranking.

- Use the job title from the job posting in your Experience section as recently as possible (and ethical). For example, it's better to have the job title in the last year than 10 years ago. That way, if HR employees limit the search results to the past year, you have a better chance of being included.

- Use the job title from the job posting as many times in your Experience section as possible (and ethical). For example, try to use it for every job title you have held.

- Apply through the company site rather than online job boards, just in case the company favors candidates who do so. Create a database of companies you intend to check for jobs on a regular basis, do an online search of "job title + city

+ year", and use aggregate sites (that crawl through and present you all job post-ings from multiple job boards).

- Familiarize yourself with the company and insert keywords related to environ-ment, corporate culture, and industry. Since these systems are highly configu-rable in their implementations (according to the company's business requirements), the best way to be optimized in these systems is to match the job posting and environment as much as possible. For more information, refer to "Know the Company Type" on page 77.

- Take the time to answer online questions carefully. When you are asked ques-tions online prior to submitting your resume (such as "Are you legally entitled to work in this country?"), ensure you take the time to answer them appropriately. These questions are automatic filters, and if you answer them incorrectly, then your resume could be ranked lower, or even be deleted without being seen.

Prepare for the Human Review

After HR employees filter the search results to a reasonable number of resumes for reviewing manually, they present them to the hiring manager, as discussed in this section.

Human Resources Review

Online job systems can only filter resumes so far. HR employees continue to filter results to a reasonable number so they can provide the short list of candidates to the hiring manager (refer to "Beating Online Job Systems—What You Need to Know" on page 79). Of course, some companies skip the HR review and resumes are sent directly to the hiring manager.

HR employees, at their discretion, may reject any resumes with obvious caution signs: employment gaps, spelling and grammar mistakes, and insufficient experience. For more information, refer to "Create Layout and Design" on page 13 and "Boost Your Content (Good Secrets to Know)" on page 45, particularly the sections on gaps.

Tip: HR employees look for ways to reject you, not bring you in.

HR employees are also interested in finding the right personality fit for the department and the corporate culture. They know the skill set and personality that already work well in the department and have a very good idea of the type of person who would complement the team. For more information, refer to "Be More Than a Brain" on page 66.

Hiring Manager Review

The last stop for your resume is the hiring manager, and/or an interview panel. The hiring manager relies on HR employees to make all the correct checks from an HR point of view.

The hiring manager is really focused on the actual skill set you have and how you will complement the team.

Tip: The hiring manager is interested in your qualifications as well as your personality fit with the team.

Here is where the words you have chosen to describe yourself will really pay off. Spend the time to create your best impression.

▶ Doing It Yourself

To ensure your resume gets through the online job systems:

- Match the job positing as closely as possible, because online job systems filter resumes based on the job posting.

- Use the exact words in the job posting, as opposed to synonyms.

- Use multiple instances of the words in the job posting for even better results.

- Use the job title provided in the job posting, if possible, as many times as you can.

- Show that you are a match for the company environment.

- Be careful when you answer online questions because they could result in instant rejection.

- Always remember that humans will eventually review your resume, and if you ignore what they need, then they will ignore you.

Using Social Media to Create an Online Presence

It is absolutely vital to have an online presence in the current market. It's no longer a nice-to-have. Many jobs are posted only on LinkedIn or other online sites, and companies are actively recruiting through social media. Consider the example of Sony Electronics, which found 25% of its candidates on LinkedIn in five months. Many employers review online profiles of potential candidates before deciding to interview them.

Key methods to creating an online presence include LinkedIn, Twitter, Facebook, and a personal website or blog. These media are increasingly used to advertise jobs, select and filter candidates, and do informal reference checks.

The easiest way to learn how to create an effective online presence is to search online for successful people in your field and see where they show up, then join those same sites (refer to "Connect with Good People" on page 92). That way, you leverage the hard work that somebody else did to boost their own profile, without doing nearly as much work.

This person could be a presenter you enjoyed at a conference, an author, an executive, or a top expert. For more information, refer to "Connect with Good People" on page 92.

Tip: Do what successful people have already done because they know what works.

Example

Here is an example of why managing your online image matters.

Razor Suleman is founder and CEO of Achievers (www.achievers.com), which helps clients build cultures of recognition that inspire employees to achieve and grow, driving results for the organization. He needed to hire 17 people in a month, so instead of advertising in newspaper ads or online job boards, he turned to social media sites.

With respect to the use of social media sites for hiring, he says, "The world has changed—it will never go back." Suleman sent job postings to his employees and these postings were redistributed through Facebook status updates, tweeting and retweeting, and LinkedIn networks. Within one week using social media sites, for these 17 positions 1000 people were expected to come to the company's open houses, according to the *Globe and Mail.*

Suleman isn't the only CEO turning to social media sites. According to the *Wall Street Journal,* New York venture-capital firm Union Square Ventures posted a job for an investment analyst but didn't want any resumes. They asked applicants to send links showcasing their online presence, such as through Twitter, Tumblr, and personal videos. "We are most interested in what people are like, what they are like to work with, how they think," says Christina Cacioppo, an associate at Union Square Ventures.

LinkedIn

LinkedIn is the most popular professional social media site. Use these LinkedIn strategies (courtesy of Jobfully and LinkedIn):

Tip: LinkedIn updates its functionality often, so check for updates.

- Profile: Complete and make public. According to LinkedIn, users with complete profiles are 40 times more likely to receive opportunities through LinkedIn.
- LinkedIn URL: Change your LinkedIn URL to your name or brand. Note that your previous URL will be invalid, so do this when you set up your profile.
- Headline section: Create an eye-catching headline section that may include your job title, brand, and top skills. Refer to leaders in your field for tips.
- Email: Include your personal email in the headline or Summary of Qualifications section so people can contact you without an introduction.
- Location: Set your location to the closest major city of where you do most of your work.
- Status: Update your status often with information that is useful to others.
- Skills: Use the LinkedIn skills feature to add skills to your profile.

- Connections: Build your network at every opportunity. As soon as you meet somebody, send them an invitation to connect on LinkedIn. Import your address book.

- Groups: Join, start, and participate in groups. Share your knowledge.

- OpenLink network: Selecting the OpenLink network badge allows anybody on LinkedIn to send you a message or job opportunity for free (no introduction or InMail is needed).

- Recommendations: Ask for recommendations as well as give them in an unsolicited way.

- Filters: Use filters to find information and people. Know that filters are also used in finding you, so make sure you enter information as recommended on LinkedIn.

- LinkedIn Learning Center: Learn how LinkedIn works for candidates and recruiters. Sign up to follow information on Twitter.

- Premium account: Consider paying for a premium account, as it provides you with some useful features such as:

  - Featured applicant: When you apply for jobs through LinkedIn, your profile will be moved to the top of the list of applicants.

  - Who viewed my profile: See who viewed your profile.

  - Contact decision makers: You can send messages to recruiters and hiring managers, even if they are outside of your network.

Twitter

Unlike some social media sites, where your messages are made available only to your contacts, Twitter as a microblogging service reaches a public audience. You may be surprised at how many jobs (and job searching tips) you can find on Twitter.

Your tweets should be professional, insightful, and helpful. Show your values through your tweets. Use the following Twitter tips (provided partially from Jobfully):

- Profile: Create a professional profile. Professional profiles are used in searches. Use job titles (for example, nouns such as "project manager") rather than verbs (for example, managing projects).

- Famous profiles: Review Twitter profiles of "famous" people in your field, and then follow what they do. Famous people are always miles ahead of everybody else in innovation, so consider using their techniques.

- Hash tags for job searching: Use a hash tag (#) for tweeting and searching. When tweeting, using a hash tag enables others to find you or your tweet, for example, #resume. When searching for a job, enter a hash tag followed by a key phrase, for example #itjobs, #SAPjobs, and #torontojobs. Be creative in the words you search for.

- Searching: Twitter makes it very easy to find professionals or areas of interest through searches. Save any of your searches for later retrieval. Know that Twitter search results rank by name, user name, and the biography on the profile. Twitter encourages users to tweet, retweet, and mention regularly so your presence is reinforced among your followers.

- Networking: Because searching on Twitter is easy, networking on Twitter is also easy. It is a great way to become connected to people you want to follow, either to learn from or work with at a future date.

- Help: See the Twitter Help Center for tips on how to use Twitter.

Facebook

At one time, Facebook was thought of as a social, not professional, site. Now, many companies and consultants have Facebook accounts. The line between professional and personal is blurring, so you always need to be aware of your overall image.

Now, it's no fun to be business-like all the time, always looking over your shoulder to make sure you don't lose job opportunities because somebody didn't like your spontaneous Facebook comment. If you are concerned about how your Facebook account may hurt your job chances, then change the privacy settings.

You could also use an alternate name just as many others have on "Fakebook". Some users prefer this cover so they can show their full selves to their friends without hurting their professional image.

There have been cases of Facebook firings, where employees posted negative comments about their bosses and were fired, with cause, so be careful.

Blogs and Websites

Blogs and websites are really great ways to show your skills, qualifications, and portfolios. If you are in a position of knowledge and experience to be able to share this information with others, then do it. Sharing knowledge can also help create the impression you are an expert, which enhances your job prospects.

▶ Doing It Yourself

To use social media effectively:

- Get a LinkedIn account and use LinkedIn tips to create a strong, professional online presence.
- Get a Twitter account.
  - Start tweeting to help other people.
  - Follow famous and relevant people.

- If you rely on Facebook for professional networking, then be careful what you post in your comments.

- If you really want to use Facebook as a social site, then consider an account with a different name.

Fix Your Online Image

If you have a great resume, but a poor online image, then you need to fix your online image.

You may have a poor online image because you posted some controversial or unprofessional comments on social media sites. Even an inconsistent image contributes to a poor online image by generating doubt and confusion. This is your branding and it needs to be positive and professional.

Tip: The key to presenting an image that gives people confidence is positive consistency.

In essence, don't say anything your grandma wouldn't be proud of seeing. You want to make sure companies are spending their time getting interested in you, not becoming doubtful or confused. Companies don't want to take a chance on hiring somebody who has a poor online image.

To learn what your online image is, search for your name and email to see what kind of image you (and people with the same name as you) are presenting. Create Google alerts for yourself.

When you join a new discussion group, review past discussions before posting a new one, just in case it has been posted already. Be sure to include a signature line with contact information in your posts. You may even decide to use an alternate user ID in some discussion forums. Also, focus on what you can *give* your network, as people who give are the ones who end up receiving.

If you or somebody else has posted socially unacceptable information about yourself, then try to have this information removed. If that is not possible, then consider using a variation of your first name or even your middle name on your resume. Be ethical, though. Senior Recruiter Sup Das advises that clients are sophisticated and will detect misleading information.

▶ Doing It Yourself

To fix your online image:

- Search for your email and name to find out what your online image looks like.

- Make sure your online image is positive and consistent (not confusing).

- Always be professional—think that your grandma and boss are reading everything.

Key Points

In this chapter, we learned:

- Resumes must be about your target audiences, not you.
- Strive to identify target audiences and their needs.
- Finding out why the job is available can enhance your chances at the resume submission stage.
- Keep an ongoing list of qualifications for jobs you want.
- People like people who are similar to them, especially in their values.
- Finding out the company type and addressing it in your resume can enhance your application.
- Create and fix your online image.

Next Steps

Now that you have learned how to move your resume to the top, let's learn techniques to keep it there. Few people ever put in the additional work to keep their resume at the top, so when you do the additional work you really have a great advantage over other people.

Keep Your Resume on Top (Ahead of the Pack)

6

If you want something you've never had before,
you must be willing to do something you've
never done before.

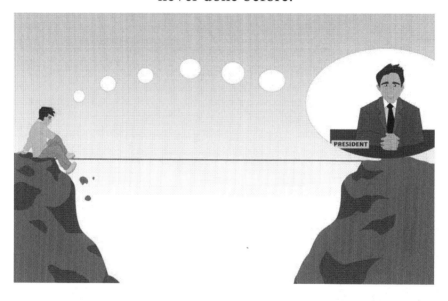

Introduction

Two friends, Ray and Andrew, both graduated from the same help desk agent program and began looking for a job. They each had different approaches for their resume with different levels of success.

Ray's Approach

Ray decided to write his resume quickly and distribute it immediately. He wrote his resume in a few days. He listed all his jobs and experience, which included volunteer soccer coach, fast-food cashier, and car wash attendant.

Ray didn't see any need for any research because, after all, he was just writing down what he did in his previous jobs. He coached soccer, served food, and worked in a car wash. His goal? He just wanted a job. He had a lot of student loans to pay back and he desperately needed a job. Ray then posted his resume to as many job boards as he could find.

Andrew's Approach

Andrew took a different approach. He desperately needed a job also, but since this was a major step in his life, he decided on a different strategy. Andrew also had unrelated jobs on his resume—volunteer firefighter, office clerk, and landscaper— so he was in a similar predicament as Ray. Still, he decided to define his goals and support his approach with research rather than blast his resume onto job boards.

Andrew reviewed 50 help desk job postings and formulated a preferred profile of a help desk agent. He had a vision of the kind of person employers wanted for experience, qualifications, education, values, and personality.

Then, he reviewed his resume and emphasized the transferrable skills that would interest an employer:

- Volunteer firefighter—Yes, he fought fires. As a help desk agent, employers are interested in other skills he had: being able to respond quickly, efficiently, and reliably; troubleshooting; working well with people; being a good communicator; and being able to follow procedures.

- Office clerk—While his job was to sort mail and perform other administrative duties, he also helped his coworkers with their computer problems, so he decided to emphasize these skills instead.

- Landscaper—Landscaping didn't seem related to computers at all, initially. When Andrew thought more about it, he realized that he could focus on his people skills: understanding and relaying customers' problems, finding solutions that fit their needs, and providing follow-up calls to verify customer satisfaction (which were statistics he kept). He also volunteered to design and implement a customer contact database for his employer. It didn't take very long, but the database looked great on his resume.

Guess Who Got the Job He Wanted

Let's see how the different approaches worked:

- Ray got a job right away working at a fast-food restaurant. He took it as a short-term measure until he got the job he wanted as a help desk agent. The problem is, he was so busy with his new job that he didn't have very much time to look for another job.

- Andrew found a job as a help desk agent after three weeks. His employer knew he was qualified on the technical side from his educational program, and the employer was impressed with how his previous experience gave him valuable skills in dealing with people.

If you want something you've never had before, you must be willing to do something you've never done before. Understand what your goals are, know the environment you're competing in, and revise your resume to meet the needs of your audiences.

In This Chapter

The topics discussed in this chapter are:

- Create Your Goals (page 92)
- Connect with Good People (page 92)
- Realize That Knowledge Is Power (page 94)
- Think and Act Creatively (page 96)
- Common Sense Points Worth Saying (page 97)

Create Your Goals

Your entire strategy flows from your goals, consciously or subconsciously. Action flows from where your thoughts are. Have you ever woken up on a Saturday morning without goals for the day? What did you get done? Maybe not much.

Tip: Resume writing and goals go together.

You need goals to set you on the right track from the beginning. Goals help define what you want and, just as importantly, what you don't want. Answer these questions for yourself:

- What job do you want?

- Do you have all the qualifications do get this job? If not, what do you need and how can you get it?

- Which companies do you want to work for?

- What type of environment do you want to be in: small startup, large company, the government, or nonprofit? Is there casual or formal dress? Are you working regular, flexible, or long hours?

- What skills and qualifications does the preferred candidate have, and how can you present the perception of an ideal candidate in your resume?

- What is your plan to achieve your goals?

If you know where you're going, then it's a lot easier to get there.

Connect with Good People

Get connected with good people who can help you, as discussed in this section.

Contact Associations and Groups

Associations and groups of all kinds tend to be advantageous networking opportunities. As a member, you can have camaraderie, support, skills development, and access to unadvertised jobs. Online discussion groups such as those on LinkedIn also offer support, knowledge, and job leads. Alumni associations are known sources of great networking, as are business associations, because you can benefit from people who have already travelled the path you want.

Choose Successful People

Choose to be around successful people, since success is known to "rub off" on other people. Attend professional association meetings, Toastmasters, and conferences. Successful people are inundated with opportunities that they can't pursue. If you demonstrate that you are of high caliber, then perhaps some of these opportunities will be offered to you. Also refer to "Common Sense Points Worth Saying" on page 97.

Get to Know the Rich and Famous

Get to know the rich and famous people in your field (or at least their work) through websites, discussion groups, reviews, and books. Read what the famous people write about trends and good practices so you know how your field is changing and the new skills you should learn. Join the same associations that they are members of—the rich and famous probably know what they're doing, and you can leverage the hard work they have done to save yourself time and effort. How do you find out which associations they are part of? Google them.

Find a Mentor

Using a mentor can be one of the best ways to jump ahead of the people lined up for a job. Mentors provide an objective viewpoint of your strengths and weaknesses, know the field, and can accelerate your growth. If you're not sure how your resume compares with your peers, then find a senior colleague, associate, or friend to give you feedback. For more information about finding a mentor, refer to "Show Appreciation" on page 99 and "Conduct Information Interviews" on page 106.

Get Personal with Hiring Managers and Recruiters

"Avoid the portal whenever you can," advises Senior Recruiter Sup Das. He says your best chance in finding a job is to make personal connections with hiring managers and recruiters, rather than apply through one of the major job boards.

Das recommends using LinkedIn, not only to expand your network, but to find a job. When you find a job you think you are qualified for, try to have coffee with the hiring manager. At the very least, find somebody who can deliver your resume personally. LinkedIn is useful in helping you find people who work at the same company.

Tip: You still need a good resume even when you avoid the portal, because eventually your resume will be read by somebody.

▶ Doing It Yourself

To get connected with good people:

- Create job and career goals. Goals help define what you want and what you don't want.

- Become a member of groups and associations.

- Become acquainted with success. Success rubs off.

- Get to know the rich and famous people in your field. Read what they do. Do what they do.

- Find a mentor who can accelerate your growth.

- Try to create personal connections with hiring managers.

- Use social media to expand your network. For more information, refer to "Using Social Media to Create an Online Presence" on page 82.

Realize That Knowledge Is Power

Many people have been credited with realizing that knowledge is power. The more you know, the more of an advantage you have in the job market, as discussed in this section.

Create a List of Qualifications for the Preferred Profile

Understanding the preferred profile enables you to create a list of qualifications that you know your target audiences want. Include experience, education, computer and technical skills, and personality traits. For more information about preferred profiles, refer to "Be the Preferred Profile (Get a Good Impression)" on page 65.

By developing this list, you will gain some information about the skills you need to obtain to be considered the preferred candidate. While you are looking for work, try to gain these skills. As an interim measure, have a plan for gaining these skills so that in the interview you are not blindsided by a question relating to your weaknesses. For more information, refer to "Education Problems and How to Fix Them" on page 36.

If your field changes quickly, review your list frequently to confirm that it is still current. You will collect this information from a number of sources, including colleagues, employers, recruiters, job postings, discussion groups, articles, blogs, and websites.

Tip: Information is everywhere—just go get it.

Note that your list may be different than your colleague's because you may have different goals and target audiences. You are a different person than your colleague. This list will also vary according to the environment you want to work in: small or large company, hardware versus software, or process-oriented versus startup (refer to "Know the Company Type" on page 77).

Tip: If you understand what the preferred profile is and present yourself that way, then your chances of getting an interview increase.

Collect Data About Prospective Employers

Collect data about prospective employers so you are continually aware of their current requirements. Scan discussion groups and online job boards for employers who hire people like you, and connect with the company on Facebook and LinkedIn.

Keep information about these employers, and review it regularly so you can identify trends in hiring from a particular sector or company. Additionally, enter this information into your personal job database.

There are several free contact databases available, but even a simple spreadsheet will help you organize your information.

Tip: Collect and organize your job data for easy retrieval.

Over time, get to know the employees of a prospective employer. Keep in regular contact with the people in your database, and continually update it with new information. Do not limit your database to strictly business information. If you have hundreds of contacts, then it will be difficult to remember every conversation. Include other bits of information that will allow you to build relationships.

For example, suppose you call one of your contacts and she mentions that she just returned from vacation and is inundated with 300 emails. The next time you speak with her, you have an immediate connection point by asking her if she has been able to deal with all those post-vacation emails. Or, you could mention that you wished that you were on vacation yourself, and mention the name of the destination she traveled to the last time you spoke. Building rapport helps people to get to know and trust you. People want to work with people they trust.

Tip: Trust is paramount in a relationship. People want to work with people they trust.

Note that people are not going to trust you just because you are a nice person. People are naturally cautious of people they don't know. I once heard somebody say, "Don't trust people until they give a reason to trust them." Focus on relationship-building skills, show you are trustworthy, be ethical, and respect them at all times. You never want to lose somebody's trust. Make a good impression and honor your words.

Pay Attention to the News

Paying attention to the news and reading it every day can provide some valuable information to help you in your job search:

- Recent contract awards: If you become aware of recent large contract awards (such as those by the federal government), then you can assume they will begin hiring people to fill the job openings. For more information, refer to "Understand the Hiring Cycle" on page 96.

- Stock prices: Stock prices may be a good indication of the financial health of a company. If they are doing well, and their stock is rising, then they are probably in a growth phase.

- New laws: New or changing standards and legal requirements can also be cues to new jobs. Keep pace with new laws (or new trends that could become laws) that force companies to make changes and hire people with your skill set.

▶ Doing It Yourself

To gain knowledge that you can use to improve your resume:

- Keep a list of qualifications that your target audiences want, and update the list often.

- Look everywhere for information and create a comprehensive list of qualifications. You should know what you have and what you need.

- Create a database of contacts. Build good relationships with your contacts through trust.

- Read business news every day to be familiar with hiring trends and upcoming opportunities.

Think and Act Creatively

Logic is great, but it's not the only thing. Successful people use their imagination and creativity to find opportunities for themselves. You can use these same techniques, as discussed in this section.

See Connections Everywhere

Your ability to see connections and create connections between seemingly disparate pieces of information can enhance your job prospects. You may not see a connection between an empty building and an accounting job opportunity until you learn that a prominent accounting firm is moving into the building. Since they are expanding their space, it is logical to assume that business is doing well and that they are in growth mode.

Realize That New Hires Don't Always Work Out

Sometimes new hires, for whatever reason, don't work out. If you interviewed for a job and was one of the final contenders, then keep in touch with HR employees. You never know when a new opportunity will come.

Understand the Hiring Cycle

If a company receives a large contract award or begins a large project, then they hire the staff in waves according to how they are needed on the project.

Observe the hiring trends for other jobs that come before you in the hiring cycle. When you see jobs for your colleagues, pay attention, as it may be a cue that your own job type will be advertised. Get ready to join the wave.

Pay Attention to the Words You Use

In recognition that words are a very powerful connector among people, pay attention to the words you use.

If you use terminology that is incorrect or not in general use, then other people may wonder if there are other issues that exist with your interpersonal communication or skills. Not using common terminology should not, in itself, be the reason you are denied a job, but it does have the predictable effect of casting doubt in a hiring manager's mind about how well you will fit in her team. If you mention that you want to start "twitting", might that give the impression you're out of touch?

Although this might not be true, it's perceptions that we're dealing with in the job market. If these points of disconnect occur several times, then you may be chipping away at their confidence in you as a candidate. It could be subtle, or it could be powerful. Avoid creating any doubt and give them every reason to have confidence in you.

▶ Doing It Yourself

To use creativity to keep your resume on top:

- See connections everywhere.
- Keep in contact with HR departments, since new hires don't always work out.
- Understand the hiring cycle for projects so you know when your specific job type may be hired.
- Be aware that words are a powerful connector (and filter) among people, and indicate knowledge and fit.

Common Sense Points Worth Saying

Some points are common sense but, nonetheless, worth saying, as discussed in this section.

Pursue Multiple Opportunities

All successful people know you don't pursue one opportunity. For a variety of reasons beyond your control, and even the company's control, a job can (and often does) fall through. Even a job that appears to be guaranteed in your favor can suddenly disappear. Pursue multiple opportunities to protect yourself from unforeseen problems. Don't consider a job officially "yours" until you have a contract signed by you and your new employer, and you have a copy of that signed document.

Example

Here is an example that illustrates the importance of pursuing multiple opportunities.

One candidate who had been looking for work for several months signed a contract with a consulting company. She was elated. She was even more elated when she arrived home and there was a message from another company that wanted to interview her. Because she had already signed a contract with the first company, and was told she would be receiving her copy of the contract the next day, she promptly returned the call and declined the interview.

Unfortunately, the next day her new boss called her and told her the job was cancelled because a major project was cancelled. She was stunned. In addition, since she rejected the second company's offer for an interview, they were no longer interested in her. She learned the hard way that until you receive a signed contract in hand, or you actually begin work, it is not "your" job.

Be Open

Some people have a very narrow view of where they want to work and exclude all other possibilities. This is not a recommended strategy because you never know where opportunity will lead. I received a call for a six-week job. I could have declined this short job, but I didn't hesitate to take it because it was a new environment, and I would essentially be getting paid to learn. As it turns out, the manager was able to keep me on the project for eight months. Be open. Also refer to "You Don't Receive a Callback After the Initial Contact" on page 112.

Know What You're Good At

There are a lot of different ways to market your resume and find a job. Filter the tips you hear for your own objectives and personality. Nobody can do this work for you, and really, nobody else knows what is best for you.

I wanted to work as a writing consultant, but wasn't very good in sales. I bought sales books, attended sales seminars, and networked. I still didn't get any better in sales. I began having trouble paying my bills and wondered if I made the wrong decision. Doing sales just wasn't my personality, and I dreaded doing it.

It wasn't that I couldn't write. I was already an accomplished writer, but that didn't make me a better salesperson. So, I decided to take a different approach. I decided to let recruiters find the work for me. They receive a percentage of my hourly rate in return for their services. This has worked out very well. I still can't sell, but I have no problem getting contracts.

Get a Personality

People do things for people they like. Now is the time to develop a knockout personality. If people close to you say you have issues to work on, then actively consider it. If several people note the same issue, then you know the issue is likely to be true.

These personal issues can hinder a job search process because people experts (such as human resources employees) are very good at sniffing out negative issues. For the sake of your own success, work on your own issues.

One of my issues that prevented me from early job success was my shyness. I was so shy I barely talked. It didn't matter that I was competent if I didn't know how to connect with people. What did I do?

I began studying social interactions in a way that somebody might study the laws of physics. I read textbooks and fine-tuned my skills in observation. I intentionally worked in the communications field after university so I could learn more about interpersonal communications (and get paid for it). My strategy worked and pulled me out of shyness into job success.

Do what you need to do in order to develop a knockout personality. Your job success depends on it.

Show Appreciation

If people give you their time to help you, be respectful and appreciative. If they give you information interviews, then have your questions and goals ready. Do your research beforehand. Be very specific, direct, and efficient. Listen to what they have to say.

Successful people have worked long hours and accumulated a significant amount of knowledge. The ones I know would be willing to share their knowledge with somebody who shows similar values: a serious person who is willing to work hard.

If they agree to meet you, then immediately suggest that you will travel to their chosen location as opposed to meeting where it is convenient for you. Treat each of these interactions like a job interview. Be respectful and professional.

Follow-up each meeting (even if it is a teleconference) with a thank-you email within one day. Not only does the thank-you note show that you appreciate their advice, it provides another opportunity for you to create a connection with them.

After university, I wrote thank-you notes to everybody who helped me find a job. Anybody who gave me one iota of advice I entered into my contact database. Even if the person only gave me another name to call, I sent a thank-you note.

I did this to, first of all, show appreciation for the time spent to help me. I also did this to create formal connections and a stronger place in their memories. The more interactions I had with them, the more they remembered me and were willing to help me. For more information about information interviews, refer to "Conduct Information Interviews" on page 106.

Example

Here is an example of why it's important to show appreciation.

I have done a lot of pro bono work helping people find jobs. Over the years, I have met hundreds of people. Some of them I never hear from again (not even a thank-you email after the meeting). These people naturally disappear from my thoughts, and I get back to my busy day. Other people send thank-you emails, and they stay afloat in my mind longer.

Still others go the extra distance and show me a gesture of appreciation through an inexpensive or free gift. They keep active in my thoughts because of the goodwill they generated. One candidate gave me tickets to a home and art show that he himself obtained for free. All he needed to do (and did) was call me two years later and introduce himself as the man who gave me the tickets, and I opened up my calendar for him. Another candidate took me out to lunch as a way to hear job advice. Still another candidate brought me a beautiful flower she picked from her own garden. It truly is the thought that counts, and gestures of appreciation really are remembered.

I am definitely not suggesting gift buying is appropriate for all situations, as some companies have strict policies over accepting a gift of any kind. As a consultant, I set my own policies in terms of what I feel is ethical: coffee, lunch, or an inexpensive (or better yet, free) gesture of appreciation.

When I applied for a marketing job, in the course of my research for the position I called a university professor at a top MBA school. I explained that I wanted to know my suitability for the position given my background, and any deficits I had that I could research before the interview (to strategize for the gaps). I asked him if I could have 10 minutes of his time. He agreed. The professor told me my deficits were primarily in pricing strategies.

A few days later in the interview, the HR person told me I wasn't fully qualified for the job. I suspected this was a test question because, I reasoned, if I'm being interviewed for the job then *somebody* thinks I'm qualified (in this case, the owner of the company). To his surprise, I readily agreed with him and told him my deficits were primarily in pricing strategies. I pointed out that the owner excelled in pricing strategies, so my deficits would not adversely impact the company. I passed the interview with no reservations.

For the university professor, I followed up our call with a handwritten thank-you note. I never needed to connect with him again, but if I did, I'm sure he would be more inclined to remember the lady who sent him a thank-you note over one who interrupted his day for 10 minutes on the phone and then disappeared. Somebody who doesn't show appreciation may be remembered in a negative way, which is worse than not being remembered at all.

Be Ethical

It is estimated that about 40% of resumes are inaccurate, says Sunny Bates, CEO of executive recruitment firm Sunny Bates Associates. Inaccuracies may be innocent omissions or intentional misrepresentations. In either case, your resume can be rejected if it is not 100% accurate.

Senior Recruiter Sup Das says you need to be perfect in every step of the hiring process. Any inaccurate information, whether intentional or not, could result in your rejection. It is a buyer's market and prospective employers have sophisticated means of verifying the accuracy of your resume.

Be ethical in all interactions that you have with people. I hope that everybody who reads this book is already ethical and realizes the value that ethics brings to the job search. Warren Buffet, CEO of Berkshire Hathaway, is known to have said that you can't make a good deal with a bad person. He also said that he looks for three qualities in a person he hires: integrity, intelligence, and energy. If they don't have the first, then the other two will be a disaster. Remember, recruiters and HR employees use databases to keep track of what you say and write—it's a permanent record.

▶ Doing It Yourself

To do the common sense tasks:

- Pursue multiple opportunities.
- Be flexible about working in a variety of companies and industries.
- Know what you're good at, and get help with what you're not good at.
- Know that people do things for people they like.
- Get a knockout personality, because great personalities lead to great opportunities.
- Appreciation can cost you nothing and yet make a significant impact.
- Be ethical.

Key Points

In this chapter, we learned:

- Creating goals is an important step to improving your resume.
- Becoming connected with people is your best chance at getting a job.
- Knowledge is power, so keep learning.
- Thinking and acting creatively can lead to a job.
- Information interviews can help improve your resume.
- Showing appreciation can help you get a job.

Next Steps

Now that you have learned several techniques to keep your resume on top, let's learn how to test and release your resume.

Test and Release

7

Getting ready to release your resume is like getting ready to release an IT system…test, test, test for bugs.

Introduction

A developer, Debbie, secluded herself in her apartment for three days to write her resume. Debbie literally stayed there until it was finished. She was so proud of what she accomplished: a new, modern resume on a single page. She reduced the size of the font to make sure that it did not exceed one page. She removed a lot of the "junk" (that is, the details) and just gave hiring managers a quick preview of herself. She would tell the hiring manager more in the interview. Debbie was very confident she would get a job within weeks.

Debbie didn't get a job. She applied for 50 jobs and didn't get any responses. She didn't understand. In her previous job, Debbie received a lot of compliments about her work and a prominent staff award. She also had a lot of responsibility. What happened?

When Debbie finally showed her resume to some human resources professionals, her resume reality began to unfold. They unleashed on her. *Too cramped. Not enough detail. Crazy format. Can't see what you can do for me. No wonder you didn't get any calls. This is a terrible resume.*

Terrible? Really?

After two months of no job hits, Debbie received one phone call for an interview.

When she arrived at the interview, the manager was already sitting down at the table. She saw her resume on the table in front of him. The manager barely started the interview when he turned her resume around, abruptly pushed it toward her, and asked, "If you were me, and you came across this resume, what would you say?"

Debbie didn't have to think for very long. She shared all the negative comments people told her. The manager sat back, listening. This is the self-criticism and awareness he wanted to hear. The interview continued and the manager, now satisfied that Debbie was fully qualified, offered her the job.

What does Debbie now do with her resume? She shows it to several people before she sends it to the hiring manager. Luckily, Debbie was able to recover from a bad resume.

Companies do not release new systems without testing them, and neither should you release your resume without fully testing it. Conduct your own testing with friends, family, and trustworthy colleagues before releasing it to online job systems and hiring managers.

In This Chapter

The topics discussed in this chapter are:

Approach to Testing and Releasing Your Resume

When you test and release your resume to prospective employers, remember to embrace criticism you receive throughout this process as knowledge you can use to improve your resume.

Understand the Power of Feedback

As a writer who has worked on collaborative projects for 20 years, I'm a big believer in the power of direct feedback from a spectrum of people, from layman reviewers to experts. The notion that nonspecialized people can provide valuable feedback in the product development process is well known in usability studies, product testing, and focus groups. For more information, refer to "Think of Yourself As a Product Looking for a Buyer" on page 10.

Do not exclude feedback just because reviewers "don't understand your field". Remember, your resume in the resume system will be seen by many people who don't fully understand your field. If you notice a trend in the feedback, then you will know the comment can generally be accepted as true.

Use Criticism to Improve Your Resume

Every successful person has faced rejection in their lives. They have learned not to take rejection personally, but use it as an opportunity to examine the problem factually and objectively, and then improve. You are going to get a better resume through criticism.

Tip: People don't know what they don't know. Find out what you don't know.

Actively seek criticism from everybody you can: employers, colleagues, friends, and family. Listen objectively and seek clarification when you don't understand. When people give you criticism, express appreciation for their time, and then decide yourself whether to accept their comments.

If your resume doesn't yield results for you yet, don't be discouraged. There could be a number of reasons why your resume isn't working yet, and perhaps none of them have anything to do with your skills. For more information, refer to "Common Problems and How to Fix Them" on page 53.

Remember, resumes are part of a system. As with any system, when it is not working, you identify the point of failure, examine the root cause, generate a solution, and then apply the fix (refer to "Learn the System" on page 7). You repeat this process until your system works, and then release your resume again.

▶ Doing It Yourself

To test and release your resume:

- Actively seek criticism.
- Don't take rejection personally.
- Identify the points of failure and fix them.
- Test your resume before you release it.
- Conduct your own tests with people you know.
- Notice trends in feedback.

Conduct Information Interviews

Information interviews can result in improvements to your resume in a number of ways. These interviews allow you to gain current information about skills and requirements needed in your field, which puts you in a better position to acquire them and enhance your resume.

Contact Experts

Become acquainted with experts in your field and leverage their expertise. Find them through professional associations, conferences, webinars, LinkedIn groups, and search engines.

Tip: Learn from successful people so you can skip some of the trial-and-error phase of learning.

Many experts remember how hard it is to start out and are very willing to spend 10 minutes with you on the phone. Start at the top of the organization and then expect to get bumped down to a less senior person. Experts are busy people, so don't be discouraged if you need to make several calls before somebody has time to talk with you.

When you contact them, be very efficient with their time. Ask them specific questions about what you are looking for, your trouble spots, and information you need.

Dig Deep into Expert Knowledge

You can use information interviews as opportunities to ask experts about their specialized knowledge or hard-to-find information related to the field:

- How did you get into this field?
- How did you learn the skills you needed for your job?
- What do you do on a typical day?
- How can somebody get started in this field?

- Considering my resume, what are the ideal skills, traits, and experience that I still need to get a job in this field?

- How do you learn more about your field (for example, industry authors and websites)?

- What are the average rates/salaries for different levels of experience?

- What are some typical interview questions and appropriate responses?

Not only are you gathering important information that will help you in building your skills, but you are also finding out important interview questions and answers. Journalists know never to rely on one source, so ask several people the same list of questions to arrive at a comprehensive understanding of the truth, which is multifaceted and subjective.

Get a Free Resume Review

Ask the experts if they would review your resume. Having expert reviews increases the number of people who are actually acquainted with your skills. They will read your resume as opposed to scanning it for 30 seconds like busy HR employees. These reviews can yield valuable information for improving your resume and increase the amount of contact that you have with an expert, which can be helpful.

Simulate On-the-Job Training

From information interviews, you can learn more about the preferred profile of a candidate for your field, job leads, trends, and on-the-job tips. The more people you talk to, the more you will know. The more you know, the more time experts are willing to spend with you. It's one of those *positive* vicious cycles.

This is not only beneficial for your resume, but for the actual interview. Sometimes an information interview can lead directly to an interview. With all the knowledge you have gathered, you will have ready-made answers for the interview questions.

Tip: Information interviews can be used for on-the-job training.

This is exactly what happened to me in my first job out of university. I had arranged a number of information interviews with senior managers in communications. I wrote down what they said, especially the jargon and buzz words. I quizzed them about what these terms meant and how they applied them in their jobs.

For example, one of the terms was "strategic communications plan". I wanted to know everything about this term. What is it? Who writes them? How are they researched? What are the measures of success?

One time I was sitting in an information interview with a senior manager when another called her office looking for me. He had heard of me from other federal government managers (I had contacted almost all of them in the city where I lived) and invited me to come upstairs for an impromptu interview.

I was so stunned I didn't even have time to generate fear. The interview was so nonstandard. He began the interview by telling me a story about how a public relations event unfolded. A senior government official flew to another part of the country for what was supposed to be a typical public event called a "meet and greet". Unfortunately, the official was blindsided by a reporter who asked a controversial question about a local issue.

The manager suddenly stopped his story and told me the event failed, and asked me how I would have planned it. By that time, I had heard so much information about this job that I immediately provided an answer:

"Before the event I would have obtained copies of all the newspapers, including local ones, and scanned all the press coverage for stories that may involve issues relating to the senior official. I would have then discussed the possible issues with the team and developed responses. I would have also briefed her before she arrived at the public event."

He became so excited at my answer, exclaiming, "That's exactly what the officer did not do!" He instantly gave me the job. Later, he told other employees he liked my confidence and I seemed to know what I was talking about!

When is it time to stop doing information interviews? The obvious answer is when you have a job. Or a better job. Or obtained the promotion you wanted. An alternate answer is when everything you have heard has been confirmed by two valid sources and not contradicted. Some people, like expert recruiter Sup Das, say maybe never.

▶ Doing It Yourself

To use information interviews to enhance your resume:

- Schedule information interviews. All information helps propel you further than you are now.

- Use information interviews as an opportunity to have your resume reviewed by experts and practice for job interviews.

- Make sure in information interviews you get information about the field, profile of the preferred candidate, job leads, trends, and on-the-job tips.

Hone Your References

Traditionally, reference checks were conducted to verify employment at the end of the hiring process. Now these checks are conducted at any point during the process, either formally or informally. As such, it is important to continually hone your references.

On your resume, you can include excerpts of recommendations, either in a separate References section or inserted where advantageous, such as the Summary of Qualifications section. You can also obtain LinkedIn recommendations and include your profile link on your resume.

Tip: Use excerpts from references on your resume if you have obtained consent.

Getting LinkedIn Recommendations

LinkedIn recommendations are powerful because all your connections can see who is willing to endorse you. Even people not connected to you can see how well you are endorsed by others because the number of recommendations you have is displayed on the public version of your profile.

Preferably, obtain LinkedIn recommendations while you are still working for your current employer or have recently finished. Remind your colleagues of the work you did, special circumstances on the project, and your notable achievements, especially if they haven't seen you for a few years. Provide unsolicited LinkedIn recommendations for your contacts and many of them will do one for you. Helping each other is what life is about.

Save Your References Time

Help your references further by offering to draft some points for them. Your references will appreciate these efforts to save time, but make sure your wording is careful as to be a helpful reminder as opposed to an expectation.

At the management level, writers are hired to draft all kinds of content for companies. As good as CEO speeches can be, many of them are written by writers, if not an entire team of experts, not CEOs. If you are not comfortable with your writing ability, then ask somebody else to write a few comments that you can ask your reference to endorse.

In addition, most managers are willing to sign letters of recommendation written for them because they are too busy. If they do not agree with the contents, then they would not sign the letters.

Groom Your References and Support Them

Groom your references by contacting them a few times a year. William Arruda, founder of Reach, a New York personal-branding company, also suggests you can set up Google alerts about your references, and then email them congratulatory notes when you learn about their good news, such as they gave a speech, or were published or promoted. Find ways to support the people who support you.

Make sure you show appreciation to your references, such as by taking them to lunch or sending a thank-you note. Also check into the company policy beforehand to avoid an awkward moment.

By following these strategies, you can better ensure they will continue to be good references for you. Senior Recruiter Sup Das notes that references for recent jobs have more value than older references.

Tip: Keep in contact with your references and keep organized. References for recent jobs are more valuable.

Common Resume Problems and Strategies

In your job search, there could be several points of failure—points where you get stuck and don't know what to do. This section describes common resume problems and strategies.

Your Resume Doesn't Get Any Attention

The first major point of failure is that your resume fails to attract any attention at all. You don't receive any phone calls or emails from recruiters or prospective employers. In my experience, most of the time this problem is remedied simply by rewriting your resume. If your resume doesn't get any attention, verify that the following problems are not the reason.

Problem 1: Your Resume Doesn't Match the Job Posting

When the words in your resume don't match the words in the job posting, your resume may be rejected for jobs that you are actually qualified for. It is imperative that you match the job posting as closely as possible. To learn how to match the job posting, refer to these sections:

- "Problem: Your Resume Doesn't Match the Job Posting" on page 53
- "Tailor Your Resume to Beat Online Job Systems" on page 73
- "Resume Section: Education" on page 34

Problem 2: Your Resume is Not Optimized for Online Searching

If you are using a resume format that can't be processed very well in online systems, then some of your experience may be overlooked. Unfortunately, this could mean that your resume may be ranked poorly and never seen by hiring managers. To learn how to optimize your resume for online searching, refer to these sections:

- "Create Layout and Design" on page 13
- "Page Length—How Long Should It Be" on page 64
- "Tailor Your Resume to Beat Online Job Systems" on page 73

Problem 3: They Can't Find the Information in Your Resume

When recruiters or prospective employers can't find the information they're looking for, or it is insufficient, your resume may be rejected. To make information in your resume easy to find, refer to these sections:

- "Boost Your Content (Good Secrets to Know)" on page 45
- "Grab Your Audience and Keep Them" on page 52
- "Make Information Easy to Find" on page 52
- "Write for Short Attention Spans" on page 52

- "Problem: You Are Shy" on page 62
- "List Multiple Contract Renewals" on page 66
- "Mention Promotions" on page 66
- "Be More Than a Brain" on page 66
- "Be Results-Oriented" on page 67
- "Tailor Your Resume to Beat Online Job Systems" on page 73

Problem 4: Your Resume Has Unexplained Gaps

There are many legitimate reasons why people have gaps on their resumes. Unfortunately, if your gap appears unusual or lengthy without any discernible reason, your resume may be rejected without you even knowing why. To understand how to mitigate the damage caused by gaps, refer to this section:

- "Problem: You Have Gaps in the Experience Section" on page 55

Problem 5: You Don't Look Like a Good Fit for the Company

Just as important (or even more important) as your qualifications is how you fit into the company's corporate culture. To understand more about how you can create confidence in hiring managers that you are a good fit, refer to these sections:

- "Show Your Values" on page 65
- "Look Like the Locals" on page 68
- "Leave Your Purple Hair at Home" on page 68
- "Common Sense Points Worth Saying" on page 70
- "Tailor Your Resume to Beat Online Job Systems" on page 73

Problem 6: You Have Too Much Unrelated Experience

When your experience appears unrelated to the job that you are applying for, your resume may be rejected. To learn how to transform your unrelated experience by focusing on transferrable skills, refer to this section:

- "Problem: You Have Too Much Unrelated Experience" on page 58

Problem 7: You Stayed Too Long at One Company

If you stay too long at one company without progress, you give a negative impression about your skills and personality. To transform these negative impressions, refer to this section:

- "Problem: You Stayed Too Long at One Company" on page 55

Problem 8: Your Resume Has Discriminatory Information

When your resume contains discriminatory information, you may be rejected without even knowing why. To learn more about discriminatory information you should omit from your resume, refer to this section:

- "Problem: Your Resume Contains Discriminatory Information" on page 62

Problem 9: You Are Too Young or Too Old

Arguably, many candidates are unfairly labeled either "too young" or "too old" for certain job positions. To deal with age discrimination, refer to these sections:

- "Problem: You Encounter Ageism" on page 61
- "Problem: You Are Labeled a "New Grad"" on page 60

Problem 10: You Don't Promote Yourself Enough

If you are too shy in your resume, then you may not be helping hiring managers understand why they should hire you. They will overlook your resume to pursue somebody who presents the information they need to make a decision. To learn how to better promote yourself, refer to these sections:

- "Choose the Right Words" on page 47
- "Create Layout and Design" on page 13
- "Boost Your Content (Good Secrets to Know)" on page 45
- "Be the Preferred Profile (Get a Good Impression)" on page 65

You Don't Receive a Callback After the Initial Contact

The second major point of failure occurs at the initial point of contact. This means you are contacted by a prospective employer, but the call doesn't result in an interview. There may be several reasons you don't receive a callback, and you should only be concerned about this point of failure if it happens to you frequently. The main reasons this point of failure occurs are:

- Poor telephone interaction: You need to have excellent telephone etiquette. One candidate said that several recruiters called him, but none of them called him back or wanted to proceed with him. He didn't know why. He had good skills, education, and experience. After some time, he realized that his open office environment was to blame. When recruiters called, he could not have a private conversation with them, so he spoke in quiet tones. The recruiters interpreted his low volume as shyness and insecurity. He was definitely not the type of candidate recruiters wanted to send to interviews. When the candidate began calling recruiters from a meeting room (or his car), he began getting callbacks for interviews.

- Lack of professionalism: You have to convey the utmost professionalism at all times. One hiring manager says he always prescreens candidates on the phone because voices are very revealing. Do they answer the call professionally, or with a "Yeah"? Do they sound full of energy and enthusiasm, or do they sound like they just had a terrible day and are waiting to unload on somebody? If the hiring manager doesn't like the tone of their voice or choice of words, then he backs himself out of the call and finds a reason to hang up. People are often unaware what the tone of their voice is conveying. Rehearse your telephone manner with people whose opinions you trust.

- Fixation with salary: Are you open to new possibilities, or do you want to discuss salary right away, even before you know about the job? Employers don't want to hire people who just care about salary. Of course salary is important, but if the "dollar demand" is the first concern out of your mouth, it's a big turnoff. First, be interested in the details of the opportunity.

- Closed to possibilities: Do you dismiss the job outright because of the location? One job I applied for meant I would have a commute of at least two hours each way. Even though I wasn't excited about the commute, I *was* excited about the prospect of working for a Fortune 500 IT company and wanted to find out if the job was enticing enough to outweigh the commute. In the interview, I learned that the entire job was virtual and I would not have any commute at all. Be open to possibilities. Also, refer to "Be Open" on page 98.

You're Not Offered a Job After the Interview

The third major point of failure occurs when you are interviewed, but not offered the job. There may be a number of reasons the employer doesn't proceed with you, so do not be concerned if this happens once in a while. Many times, the reasons have nothing to do with the candidate—for example, the project is delayed or cancelled. Nevertheless, strive for a high success rate like some of the star candidates who are your competition.

Tip: Senior Recruiter Sup Das notes that your track record of employment matters the most, and actually determines whether you are a candidate of high quality.

After the interview, immediately write down the questions they asked you as well as your answers, and then share them with trusted colleagues and mentors. Try to note any points of disconnect or downward momentum that occurred in the interview.

If you were not the successful candidate, then make attempts to find out why. Some employers will give you cues if you ask them in a way that doesn't throw them into a legal quagmire. Rather than demand to know why you weren't hired, you could earnestly ask what the successful candidate had that the employer liked, or skills that would have enhanced your candidacy.

▶ Doing It Yourself

To fix problems with your strategy:

- Ask other people what your problems could be.

- Create a strong initial contact—it can influence whether you are invited for an interview.

- Don't be too hard on yourself if you don't get the job. There may be many reasons you didn't get the job, possibly having nothing to do with you.

- Do a proper debrief to find solutions.

Value Yourself

As has been discussed throughout this book, the impression you generate for other people is pivotal in attaining job success.

Be careful of how you present yourself. Do not be shy. Do not ever downgrade your experiences or pass them off as chance.

Sometimes you are given new responsibilities just because the guy in the other cubicle is lazy. You wouldn't be given the work if they didn't think you could do it. Choose words that value your contributions and skills. Don't let people take that away from you. Most of all, don't take that away from yourself. You earned it.

When I started in the technical writing field many years ago, I was changing fields from communications and, understandably, didn't know very much about technical writing. A company that paid less than the market average was willing to take a chance on me. I accepted the job because it was my first step into the field and I didn't have a lot of choices.

The manager was going on leave and decided to delegate management of the team to myself and another senior writer. We were both new, but he had never managed people. Over time, the entire department was stressed out by his management style and threatened to quit. He suddenly left the company. At that time, I was given the responsibility of managing the entire department and all the consultants, about 15 people.

I worked day and night learning about technical writing. During the evenings, weekends, and holidays, I had read every technical writing book in the department's library within six months. Many times I was even a bit embarrassed about how eager I was and didn't log the hours in the time sheet system. I wanted to show them that they made a good decision by giving me the responsibility.

This additional effort was noticed at the executive level. When my manager returned to her job and I had to return to my old, boring job, the vice president of operations told me to find any job in the company I wanted, and he would make it happen. If the job I wanted didn't exist, then he would create it.

Now, I could have downgraded my time as acting manager of the department in my resume and interviews. I could have said, "Because somebody left the company, I ended up managing the department." Instead, I said, "I was new to the field and within six months I was managing an entire department of technical writers."

When you work hard, take full credit for your accomplishments. You deserve to have hard work recognized.

▶ Doing It Yourself

To value yourself:

* Be aware that you can be your best friend or worst enemy with respect to generating impressions.
* Choose positive words to create positive impressions.
* Always be aware of how you create positive or negative impressions of yourself.

Key Points

In this chapter, we learned:

* Testing your resume is important to do before you release it.
* Specific techniques of appreciation can be used to hone your references.
* Every resume problem has a matching solution.
* Valuing who you are can improve your resume.

Next Steps

Now that you have learned how to test and release your resume for success, you have completed all the necessary steps in the resume writing system. Congratulations, your resume is ready to be released to prospective employers.

A Final Word 8

You have reached the finish line.

Congratulations, You Did It!

Congratulations, you have reached the finish line of the resume writing system.

Using the techniques in this book, you have learned some of the best ways to write your resume so it gets noticed by prospective employers.

Remember, a resume is never "complete" but an ever-evolving document that is tailored to meet the needs of audiences, both human and system.

Need More Help?

If you need more individual or specialized help with your resume or career, then find it at www.beatresumesystems.com.

Appendix A: Strong Verbs for Resumes

The following list of strong verbs for resumes is provided courtesy of Boston College.

Tip: To understand how to use these strong verbs in your resume, refer to "Replace Weak and Vague Verbs" on page 48.

Technical Skills

assembled	maintained
built	operated
calculated	overhauled
computed	programmed
designed	remodeled
developed	repaired
devised	solved
engineered	trained
fabricated	upgraded

Research Skills

clarified	interpreted
collected	interviewed
critiqued	investigated
diagnosed	organized
evaluated	reviewed
examined	summarized
extracted	surveyed
identified	systematized
inspected	

Financial Skills

administered

allocated

analyzed

appraised

audited

balanced

budgeted

calculated

computed

developed

forecasted

managed

marketed

planned

projected

reconciled

researched

Management Skills

administered

analyzed

assigned

attained

chaired

contracted

consolidated

coordinated

decreased

delegated

developed

directed

evaluated

executed

improved

increased

organized

oversaw

planned

prioritized

produced

recommended

reviewed

scheduled

strengthened

supervised

Communication Skills

addressed

arbitrated

arranged

authored

corresponded

developed

directed

drafted

edited

enlisted

formulated

influenced

interpreted

lectured

mediated

moderated

motivated

negotiated

persuaded

promoted

publicized

reconciled

recruited

spoke

translated

wrote

Clerical or Detailed Skills

approved

arranged

catalogued

classified

collected

compiled

dispatched

executed

generated

implemented

inspected

monitored

operated

processed

purchased

recorded

retrieved

screened

specified

systematized

tabulated

validated

Creative Skills

acted

conceptualized

created

designed

developed

directed

established

fashioned

founded

illustrated

instituted

integrated

introduced

invented

originated

performed

planned

revitalized

shaped

Helping Skills

assessed

clarified

coached

counseled

demonstrated

diagnosed

educated

expedited

facilitated

familiarized

guided

referred

rehabilitated

represented

Teaching Skills

adapted

advised

clarified

coached

communicated

coordinated

developed

enabled

encouraged

evaluated

explained

facilitated

guided

informed

initiated

instructed

persuaded

set goals

stimulated

Appendix B: Resume Checklist

Make sure you consider the following points in your resume:

---

1 **Layout and design is professional, and information is easy to find.**

Refer to:
- "Create Layout and Design" on page 13
- "Boost Your Content (Good Secrets to Know)" on page 45
- "Keep Your Resume on Top (Ahead of the Pack)" on page 89

---

2 **Resume is tailored to each job posting and company.**

Refer to:
- "Problem: Your Resume Doesn't Match the Job Posting" on page 53
- "Problem: You Have Too Much Unrelated Experience" on page 58
- "Tailor Your Resume to Beat Online Job Systems" on page 73
- "Show Your Values" on page 65
- "Look Like the Locals" on page 68
- "Leave Your Purple Hair at Home" on page 68
- "Common Sense Points Worth Saying" on page 70
- "Tailor Your Resume to Beat Online Job Systems" on page 73

---

3 **Resume is optimized for online searches.**

Refer to:
- "Page Length—How Long Should It Be" on page 64
- "Tailor Your Resume to Beat Online Job Systems" on page 73

---

4 **Education is sufficient.**

Refer to:
- "Resume Section: Education" on page 34

---

5 **Gaps are addressed.**

Refer to:
• "Problem: You Have Gaps in the Experience Section" on page 55

6 **Statements serve a purpose, are results oriented, and add to the profile of a preferred candidate.**

Refer to:
• "Boost Your Content (Good Secrets to Know)" on page 45
• "Keep Your Resume on Top (Ahead of the Pack)" on page 89

7 **Statements are accurate and objective as opposed to subjective.**

Refer to:
• "Boost Your Content (Good Secrets to Know)" on page 45

8 **Words are positioned strategically using strong action verbs and adjectives.**

Refer to:
• "Boost Your Content (Good Secrets to Know)" on page 45
• "Appendix A: Strong Verbs for Resumes" on page 119

9 **All problems are addressed.**

Refer to:
• "Common Resume Problems and Strategies" on page 110
• "Common Problems and How to Fix Them" on page 53

10 **Resume is checked for spelling and grammar.**

Refer to:
• "Check Spelling and Grammar" on page 70

Bibliography

Boston College website. "Resume Action Verbs." www.bc.edu, April 2012.

Das, Sup. Senior recruiter. Personal interviews and emails, April 2012.

Gibson, Jodi. Senior staffing consultant. Personal interviews and emails, April 2012.

Grant, Tavia. "Tweet-tweet: Want ads singing a new tune." GlobeAdvisor.com, November 12, 2009.

Jobfully website. www.jobfully.com, April 2012.

Case Study Sony Electronics. LinkedIn website, 2011.

Molisani, Jack. Personal emails and presentation *Resume Secrets that Might Surprise You*, May 2012.

Monster website. www.monster.ca, April 2012.

Schaffer, Karen. *The Complete Book of Resumes*. Sourcebooks, 2005.

Silverman, Rachel Emma. "No More Resumes, Say Some Firms." *The Wall Street Journal*, January 24, 2012.

Spiro, Michael. http://michaelspiro.wordpress.com, May 2012.

Workopolis website. www.workopolis.ca, March 2012.

Twitter website. www.twitter.com, March 2012.

Acknowledgements

I gratefully acknowledge the assistance of the following people in the development of this book:

- My students, who reviewed the initial content, provided valuable insight into what newcomers to the job market need—I learn from you. In order of first name, I would like to thank Farah Fatima, Norris Crossley, Patti Cruickshank, Shelley Therriault, and Tracey Grozier.

- Sup Das, a senior recruiter, provided a thorough quality edit of the entire manuscript. His experience in working with candidates was invaluable to the quality of this book. He provided comments that only somebody at the top of his game could do.

- Robert Long, a friend, skilled writer and editor, took the time to read this book line by line. I greatly appreciate his willingness to discuss new ideas for the book and provide honest, thoughtful feedback.

- Jodi Gibson, a senior staffing consultant who is highly regarded among his clients for obvious reasons, provided valued comments from the combined perspective of working with clients and candidates.

- Paul Stockton, a friend, programmer, and talented writer himself, provided insights that enhanced these perspectives throughout the book.

- Charles the tester, a friend and IT expert, excelled in pointing out the "what if" scenarios. In doing so, he improved the quality of this book and my own "what if" abilities.

- Rhys Griffiths, a colleague, friend, and quintessential writer and editor, provided the original template for my books. I truly savor your fine intellect and writing abilities.

- Andrew Brooke, past president of the Toronto Society for Technical Communication and a blogger worth reading, gave tips that enhanced the usability of the content.

- My friends, who have given me support and encouragement. In order of first name, I would like to thank: Andrew, Angela, Daphne, Dave, Debbie, Ellen, Jonelle, Katharine, Lesley, Mary, Nick, Paul, Ray, Raymond, Siobhan, Ted, and Ursula.

- Welton, thank you for coming into my life at the "write" time, and encouraging me to be me.

About the Author

Pamela Paterson gained an insider's edge into how online job systems work when she was part of a team that implemented a job applicant system for a global financial auditing company. She has taught about the art and science of creating effective resumes for over 15 years at workshops, colleges, and conferences.

When she is not admiring great resumes, Pamela spends her time as a consultant, college instructor, and speaker (www.writertypes.com).

She has a bachelor's degree in journalism and a master's degree in science from the University of Maryland. Pamela was inducted into the same honor society as Jimmy Carter, Hillary Rodham Clinton, and Linus C. Pauling.

Index

23643058R00083

Made in the USA
Charleston, SC
31 October 2013